PLANTS

Ballantine Books

Ballantine Books
A division of Random House of Canada Limited
1265 Aerowood Drive
Mississauga, ON L4W 1B9

INFACT Publishing Ltd.
66 Portland St., 2nd Floor
Toronto, ON M5V 2M8

CTV Television Network Ltd.
250 Yonge St., 18th Floor
Toronto, ON M5B 2N8

Canadian Cataloguing in Publication Data

Cullen, Mark, 1956—
          Plants
(Mark Cullen's Complete gardener series)
Accompanied by video.
Includes index.
ISBN 0-345-39832-7

1. Plants, Cultivated.   2. Gardening.   I. Title.   II. Series:
Cullen, Mark, 1956— . Mark Cullen's Complete gardener
series.

SB405.C85 1996   635.9   C96-930028-X

PHOTOS: Janet Davis—p.7, 9, 12, 15, 16, 19, 25, 31, 36, 40,
    43, 44, 49, 51, 54, 59, 60, 63, 64, 69, 75, 77, 79, 83, 84, 88,
    90, 94
SENIOR EDITOR: Wendy Thomas
HORTICULTURAL EDITOR: Denis Flanagan
COPY EDITOR: Sylvia Gilchrist
CTV CO-ORDINATOR: Glen Dickout, Manager, Special Projects
PROJECT MANAGER: Susan Yates, INFACT Publishing
COVER AND TEXT DESIGN AND ILLUSTRATION ART: ArtPlus:
    Brant Cowie, Dave Murphy and Jerry Stapley
SPECIAL THANKS: Dan Matheson, Canada am; Jean and John
    Farintosh; Aunt Charlotte and Uncle Tom; Len Cullen,
    my Dad; and especially, Mary for her help and support.

M+M Communications, Unionville, ON is the publishing
imprint of Mary and Mark Cullen.

Printed and bound in Canada by Metropole Litho Inc.

TABLE OF CONTENTS

• •

INTRODUCTION

"What exactly do you do?" I am sometimes asked, in reference to my "day job." My response to that is to suggest that my professional goal in life is to remove the hocus-pocus, or the barriers, that Canadians imagine stand between them and success in the garden.

This book and video are a natural extension of what I do with great passion every day. My intent is to show you how to get the most out of your garden and to do it by minimizing the "work" (maintenance) and maximizing what I believe to be the most pleasurable aspects of gardening, including lounging around the yard in a favourite chair or hammock.

My good friend Dan Matheson is no gardening dummy. Truth is, he is a fast learner with more enthusiasm than most of us can imagine. He also has a habit of asking the very questions that Canadian gardeners (and non gardeners!) have on their minds at the time. I think you will enjoy this book and video as we simplify gardening and help you to get the most from your Canadian garden through *The Complete Gardener*.

In this volume, I'll explain how you can get the most from a wide range of plants, with suggestions of how to use them in the garden. Whether you're looking for a fast-growing vine to cover an unattractive wall or ideas for balcony containers, you'll find them here. And we'll have a look at some specialty gardens — rock gardens, herb gardens, cottage gardens — and the types of plants most often associated with them.

MARK CULLEN

ANNUALS

nnuals are wonderful for their variety of colours and continuous blooms throughout the growing season. Although I try to plan my perennial beds and borders so that something is always in bloom, this may be difficult for you if you have a small urban or suburban garden. There is often not the space to grow the variety of perennials and shrubs that will keep a garden in continuous and changing colour. This is where annuals will come to your rescue — why neglect the charms of such stalwart performers as pansies, petunias, and cosmos?

Annuals are plants that complete their growing cycle in one season and are a wonderful addition to any garden. They bloom for long periods; they fill in dead spaces in the border; they are the shining stars in hanging baskets, window boxes, and other container plantings; they are inexpensive and easy to grow; and they come in a wide range of colours and heights.

Some annuals can be used as ground covers, vines, and climbers. I've included ground cover and climbing annuals in the chapters dealing with those uses. In the plant listings, I am using the informal name of the plant but including the

Latin name so that you can be absolutely sure of the plant's identification.

The list of plants that follows is by no means exhaustive. There are hundreds of annuals to choose from but, with some difficulty, I've picked out some of my favourites. They are easy to grow, they fit into many gardening situations, and many do well in containers and hanging baskets. I have also thrown in a couple of less well-known annuals. They might be a little more difficult to find, but the hunt is part of the fun of gardening. If you have trouble finding some of these plants in your garden centre, you might have better luck finding them as seeds.

BUYING ANNUALS

Plants should look fresh and compact. Avoid the leggy ones.

It is best to buy plants that are not in flower, ideally, not even with buds. Flowering plants suffer from shock when they're transplanted, and it can take quite a bit of time to start flowering again.

PLANTING ANNUALS

Keep newly purchased plants out of direct sunlight and keep them moist until you are ready to plant.

Plant seedlings when all danger of frost is past and when the soil is warm.

Plant when the sky is overcast, if possible, but if you must plant on a sunny day, try to provide shade for the newly planted seedlings. Putting an inverted basket over the plant will provide shade and still allow air movement.

Portulaca, p. 13, also known as Moss Rose, is a lovely, brightly flowered self-seeding annual.

❀ Work a 6-12-12 fertilizer into the soil of the bed.

❀ Dig a hole just big enough for the plant. When the plant is put in the hole, the soil should be at the same depth on the stem as it was in the flat or pot you've just taken it from.

❀ Add a generous quantity of compost or composted cattle manure to the planting hole and tamp the soil firmly around the seedling.

❀ If the plant has been grown in a peat pot, tear the pot partly open before planting. Make sure the peat pot is entirely covered with soil when you plant it.

❀ Water generously with a gentle spray. Add 5-15-5 transplanter fertilizer to the water. Keep the soil damp but not soaked.

RULE OF THUMB:

Soak the root mass while in the container with a 5-15-5 water solution and I guarantee a fast start for all new, young plants in your garden. The butalic acid in this fertilizer will help to encourage new feeding roots quickly.

CARING FOR ANNUALS

❋ Pinching off the growing tips of young annuals will encourage them to become bushier and produce more blooms.

❋ As they grow, stake plants that will become tall and in need of extra support.

❋ Most annuals grow well in soil that is rich in humus and well-drained. I'll note special soil needs in the plant lists that follow. As well, any special watering requirements are noted.

SOME USEFUL ANNUALS

WAX BEGONIAS   *Begonia semperflorens*
Good in shade or sun; easy care

A good plant for hanging baskets. Also a great plant for people who vacation during the growing season because it doesn't mind if the soil dries out between waterings.

COLOURS: Shades of pink, white, and red; delicate flowers
HEIGHT: 30 cm (12 inches)
LIGHT REQUIREMENTS: Full sun or light to partial shade
FERTILIZER: 20-20-20 every two weeks
PINCHING/DEADHEADING: Pick off green seed pods to encourage more bloom
USES: Looks beautiful planted in masses, in raised beds and containers, and as a border plant.
COMPANIONS: Other begonias, lobelia, alyssum, ageratum

COSMOS   *Cosmos bipinnatus*   **Easy care**

Tall with delicate, feathery foliage and daisy-like flowers on long wiry stems. A graceful addition to the back of any border or bed.

COLOURS: Red, white, pink, lavender and orange with tufted yellow centres

HEIGHT: 90 cm to 150 cm (3 to 5 feet)
LIGHT REQUIREMENTS: Full sun
FERTILIZER: None necessary
PINCHING/DEADHEADING: Deadhead only to prevent it spreading its copious seeds
USES: Makes excellent cut flowers
COMPANIONS: Snapdragons, baby's breath, zinnias

....

DIANTHUS (Pinks)   *Dianthus chinensis*
Scented flowers

Cheerful frilly flowers with a mild spicy scent; does best in fertile soil.

COLOURS: Pink, white, red, and blue, with attractive grey-green foliage
HEIGHT: 17 cm to 60 cm (7 to 24 inches)
LIGHT REQUIREMENTS: Full sun or afternoon shade
FERTILIZER: No special needs
PINCHING/DEADHEADING: Snip faded blooms for further growth
USES: Excellent cutting flower; good in beds or containers
COMPANIONS: Baby's breath, cosmos, carnations

Cosmos is a tall plant best suited for the back of the border or flower bed.

GERANIUM   *Pelargonium hortorum*
Containers, hanging baskets; easy care

An annual that is a perennial favourite! Bring zonal varieties indoors over winter.

COLOURS: Red, pink, orange, salmon, white
HEIGHT: Can grow to 60 cm (2 feet)
LIGHT REQUIREMENTS: Full sun
FERTILIZER: 15-30-15 every two weeks
PINCHING/DEADHEADING: Snip off faded flowers down to the stem
USES: Ivy geraniums — use in hanging baskets. Put upright geraniums in any pot or container.
COMPANIONS: Dusty miller and lobelia; red geraniums look dramatic with yellow marigolds

IMPATIENS   *Impatiens wallerana*
Excellent in shade, easy care

Irresistible flowers that are happiest in the shade; bloom until first frost.

COLOURS: Red, white, pink, purple, orange, salmon
HEIGHT: 30 cm to 60 cm (12 to 24 inches)
LIGHT REQUIREMENTS: Partial to full shade
FERTILIZER: 20-20-20 every two weeks (makes a big difference!)
PINCHING/DEADHEADING: Not necessary
USES: Front of shady border, containers in shady porches, balconies, or verandahs
COMPANIONS: Blue lobelia with white impatiens is stunning

LOBELIA   *Lobelia erinus*   **Easy care**

Make sure you get the correct variety for your purpose: the blue or white bush or upright form is best in borders; the trailing form has no equal in a container or hanging basket. Keep soil moist but not soggy.

COLOURS: White, purple, pink but most popular is
  deep blue
HEIGHT: Uprights grow to about 15 cm (6 inches),
  trailers to 30 cm (12 inches)
LIGHT REQUIREMENTS: Full sun or partial shade
FERTILIZER: 20-20-20 every two weeks
PINCHING/DEADHEADING: Cut plants back when they
  begin to look scraggly in middle of summer for second growth
USES: Good edging plant, fabulous in containers
COMPANIONS: Dark blue is stunning with white flowers such as white lobelia, impatiens or dusty miller;
  in sun, plant with yellow or gold French marigolds

LOVE-IN-A-MIST *Nigella damascena*
An old-fashioned flower

A great name for a great flower! Its interesting
blossoms with their clear colours offset many
brighter flowers. Another easy-to-grow self-seeder.

COLOURS: Blue, pink, white
HEIGHT: 45 cm to 60 cm (18 to 24 inches)
LIGHT REQUIREMENTS: Full sun
FERTILIZER: 5-10-5 monthly light applications
PINCHING/DEADHEADING: Seedpods are attractive but
  keep pinching to encourage more flowering
USES: In border, as cut flowers; seedpods are used in
  dried arrangements
COMPANIONS: Blue shades look fabulous next to bright
  red salvia

MONKEY FLOWER *Mimulus luteus*
Excellent in shade, poorly drained soil,
and a cool environment

If you have trouble finding this at the garden centre, seeds are available for grow-it-yourself gardeners. It's a plant that needs frequent watering.

Cuttings taken in the fall will flower indoors in the winter.

COLOURS: Yellow, orange, red, brown, cream, purple, blue; usually attractively splotched
HEIGHT: 30 cm (12 inches)
LIGHT REQUIREMENTS: Prefers shade, tolerates some sun
FERTILIZER: 20-20-20 every two weeks
PINCHING/DEADHEADING: Pinch back hard in mid-summer when it can become leggy
USES: Ground cover, edging, house plant, hanging baskets, rock gardens, pool edge; good on north-facing patio or balcony
COMPANIONS: In baskets and window boxes: lobelia, ivy, fuchsia

....

| PANSY | *Viola species* | **Easy to grow** |

One of the earliest plants that can go out in the spring and one that will bloom all season long! I've seen their cheerful faces peeping through late-season snow in Ontario. On the West Coast, February isn't too early for these hardy charmers to be put out.

COLOURS: Solids and mixtures of yellow, blue, purple, wine, maroon, orange, apricot, white
HEIGHT: 15 cm to 22 cm (6 to 9 inches)

The 'Purple Wave' petunia is a 1995 All America Selections winner.

LIGHT REQUIREMENTS: Full sun in spring, partial shade in summer

FERTILIZER: 20-20-20 every two weeks

PINCHING/DEADHEADING: Pinch back and pick regularly to keep blooming and stop legginess

USES: In beds, pots; good cut flowers

COMPANIONS: Petunia, alyssum, ageratum

PETUNIAS   *Petunia hybrida*   **Easy to grow**

Don't take the faithful petunia for granted. Recent introductions offer a wide range of colours, which get better and more varied every year. Petunias make perfect companions for just about any plant you care to partner it with. Especially attractive are the ones with deeper coloured throats.

COLOURS: All shades of blue, white, red, purple, yellow, rose, salmon

HEIGHT: 25 cm to 35 cm (10 to 14 inches)

LIGHT REQUIREMENTS: Full sun

FERTILIZER: 20-20-20 every two weeks

PINCHING/DEADHEADING: Pinch back to 15 cm (6 inches); after first bloom, cut back again. This will delay bloom but will produce bushier growth and more flowers.

USES: Borders, raised beds, containers, hanging baskets; good cut flower

COMPANIONS: Lobelia, dusty miller, geraniums

PORTULACA (Moss Rose)   *Portulaca grandiflora*

Dry sunny spots; easy care

A handy plant that grows where many other plants won't, such as very dry areas — and it self-seeds! Needs average to sandy soil.

COLOURS: Red, orange, yellow, white, coral

HEIGHT: 15 cm (6 inches)

LIGHT REQUIREMENTS: Full sun; flowers close on overcast days

FERTILIZER: None needed except when growing in containers, then use 15-30-15 every two weeks
PINCHING/DEADHEADING: Not necessary
USES: Around patios, between stones in walk, also good in beds, edgings, and rock gardens
COMPANIONS: Alyssum and vinca

DISEASES AND INSECTS

I could write a whole book on diseases and insects! To cover just a few in this book might be misleading. As most gardeners aren't interested in diseases and insects until their plants are attacked, I am going to take the easy way out and suggest that you talk to a professional at your local garden centre when you need help.

CONTAINER GARDENING

Have you ever put a geranium in a pot and set it out on your balcony or patio? A growing (excuse the pun!) number of people love growing plants in pots, basins, hanging baskets, troughs, window boxes, wall baskets, urns, strawberry pots, planters, old rubber boots (I kid you not!), wheelbarrows, wooden boxes, copper tubs, wicker baskets — in fact, anything that will hold soil and plants.

Container gardening is not necessarily easy-care gardening because of the need for constant watering, even for plants that are generally considered easy care. But, here are some suggestions to maximize the pleasure you will get from container grown plants:

Most containers will need watering daily and more often in hot windy weather. Some containers may not need daily watering but should be checked every day to assess their needs. To ensure that the soil will not dry out too quickly, especially in moss-lined hanging baskets, mix water-saving polymer crystals in with the planting soil (trade names: Soil Moist, Water Power and others). Every time you water, the crystals absorb the moisture and release it slowly. As a bonus, it improves aeration of the soil.

Container planting is often intensive planting — there are many plants competing for a limited amount of nutrients. Add granular slow-release 14-14-14 fertilizer, which is released when the plants are watered.

Use a specially prepared patio mix or container mix. These "soilless" mixes hold moisture, and reduce the potential for diseases.

Regularly deadhead the plants that need it to keep them blooming. Cut back trailers such as lobelia when midsummer takes the steam out of them. They will return with new growth. In an intensively planted container, such hard pruning won't be noticed.

Lobelia is a perfect trailing plant for container gardening.

Just as you mulch your beds and borders, you can mulch container plantings. Choose the material that is appropriate — large bark chips are out of place, but finely shredded bark or leaves will do, as will chopped pine needles or cocoa shells (a chocolatey aroma will pervade the garden for a week or so after using cocoa shells). Succulents look best set off with a mulch of fine gravel, fulfilling both horticultural and aesthetic needs.

Small plants planted at the base of larger ones can act as a mulch. For example, a froth of baby's tears or alyssum spilling out of a pot that contains an upright plant, such as dracaena, softens the edges of the container and makes the planting more attractive.

How to Use Containers

One of the reasons container planting is so popular is that it is flexible and versatile. It offers great possibilities for experimenting — mixing and matching colours, heights, textures — and it

Potted flowers offer flexibility and versatility and like these geraniums, can bring colour to an otherwise drab corner.

makes gardening in small spaces possible. Due to its accessibility, it is also good for the elderly and people with disabilities that prevent them from regular gardening. Need I go on? Here are some ideas for using containers in the garden.

❀ Plant a stunning specimen on its own in a container and place it where it will become the focal point.

❀ Use groups of pots to camouflage a permanent or temporary eyesore.

❀ Plant scented plants in containers so they can be moved around to your favourite sitting areas. Leave them in the sun for the day but move them to the patio or gazebo in the late afternoon or early evening to enjoy their scent as you relax.

❀ Use containers filled with shade-loving plants down a paved walkway between houses.

❀ Balconies are made for containers. Arrange them to provide privacy; to grow your own leaf lettuce, tomatoes, and herbs; to give afternoon shade. They are more likely to suffer from intense wind and sun the higher you go, but awnings and lattice will help protect them.

❀ Window boxes aren't restricted to windows. Attach them to deck railings, to the sides of a garage, sheds, porch, or wall.

FOLIAGE AND TEXTURE   Plants grown only for their foliage, either on their own or with other plants, add interest and drama to plantings. Try some of the following.

❀ BAY: Long, leathery, aromatic leaves; tall growing; can be pruned as topiary specimen; full or partial sun

✽ **COLEUS:** Useful for any colour scheme, leaves are multicolour in any combination of white, green, pink, red, brown, orange; shade

✽ **DUSTY MILLER:** Lovely silver leaves look great with blue and white arrangements; add a spot of red, such as a scarlet trailing geranium

✽ **MAIDENHAIR FERN:** Grows in spreading clumps; water regularly but don't overwater; withstands heavy shade

✽ **POLKA-DOT PLANT:** Gives height to a planting; bicolour foliage is any two of pink, white, green, or burgundy; shade

SCENT Some of these plants have scented flowers; others release their scent when their leaves are brushed.

✽ **DIANTHUS:** Spicy scent reminiscent of cloves; sun

✽ **NICOTIANA OR FLOWERING TOBACCO:** Sweet scent is released at night; partial shade; choose shorter varieties for container plantings

✽ **HELIOTROPE:** Sweet fragrance somewhat like vanilla; full sun

✽ **LAVENDER:** Smells like — lavender!; perennial in milder zones of the country; full sun

✽ **SCENTED GERANIUMS:** Scents include lemon, rose, apple, cinnamon, and wintergreen; sun

✽ **STOCK:** Sweet and spicy fragrances; full sun

✽ **THYME:** Small, low-growing herb; full sun

TRAILING PLANTS Tumbling over the edge of a container or cascading from a hanging basket, any of these will add a softness and lush look to your planting.

Dianthus is a sun-loving annual that has a spicy scent.

❀ **BLACK-EYED SUSAN VINE:** Climbs or tumbles depending on circumstances; flowers white, yellow, orange with dark throats; full sun to partial shade

❀ **BROWALLIA:** Star-shaped blue, white or lavender flowers; does well in shade

❀ **IVY:** Great varieties in solid greens as well as variegated; shade

❀ **IVY GERANIUM:** Shades of red, pink, white; full sun to partial shade

❀ **LICORICE PLANT:** Grey furry leaves and arching stems; good in sunny exposed conditions and by the sea

❀ **MORNING GLORY AND MOONFLOWER:** Usually seen climbing up but will trail nicely out of a large container; moonflowers in white, morning glories in blue, white, purple, crimson; sun

❀ **SWEDISH IVY:** Usually used as a house plant, makes a nice addition to containers; partial shade

❀ **TRAILING LANTANA:** Bears clusters of rosy-lilac flowers all summer long; sun or light shade

PLANTS FOR WINDOW BOXES OR STONE TROUGHS
Alpine and rock-garden plants do well in containers and many will over-winter outdoors if planted in containers that won't crack in low temperatures. If you are concerned about the plants, store the planter in a shed or unheated garage, or tuck dried leaves or evergreen branches around them.

AUBRETIA: mat-forming perennial with trailing branches bearing lilac, purple, red, or pink flowers; sun

BELLFLOWER (*Campanula*): white, blue, purple bell-shaped flowers; forms clumps; sun or partial shade

HENS AND CHICKENS: evergreen succulent that forms rosettes; gives nice texture and colour; sun

SAXIFRAGA: cushion-shaped growth, small to large sprays of flowers in yellow, white, pink, red; sun

Impatiens is always a popular choice for container plantings.

COMBINATIONS   Try these in window boxes or other containers. Match the colour scheme of the container and its plantings to be in keeping with your other plantings and with the exterior colours of your house — the siding, window frames, shutters, and so forth.

❀ Red salvia, soft yellow marigolds, silver dusty miller, and white periwinkle

❀ Fern, white wax begonia, variegated ivy, caladium (shade)

❀ White, pink begonias with blue browallia

❀ Licorice plant, which has grey-green foliage, yellow-green flowering tobacco, and blue and white bell-flowers

❀ Two clipped conifers at either end of a rectangular planter, with a variegated ivy between them — a rather formal composition

❀ Red geraniums, red and pink zinnias, yellow marigolds, and asparagus fern

THE FOUR-SEASON WINDOW BOX

SPRING: The easiest way to get a shot of early spring colour is with potted plants that are just about to bloom. Sink the plants into the window box and fill in the spaces with soil or peat moss. Some combinations to try: Tulips with pansies; grape hyacinth with primroses; crocuses, iris reticulata, variegated ivies; grape hyacinth, pansies, ivy; add evergreen boughs or miniature conifers to any of these groupings to complete the picture. The bulbs would have to be ones you had potted in the fall specifically for early spring blooms.

SUMMER: When the spring flowers have finished, remove the pots. Bulbs can be stored for planting in the garden in autumn. There's an embarrassment of riches in the summer — these suggested combinations are just a few: petunias, nasturtiums, and ivy geraniums, variegated ivy; heliotrope, petunias, licorice plant; begonias, trailing lobelia, impatiens for a shady situation; ornamental grass, variegated ivy, and caladiums for a spectacular non-flowering container in dappled shade.

FALL: Many annuals will still be suitable for the window box, but add some of these fall winners: chrysanthemums; sedum 'Autumn Joy'; ornamental peppers; ornamental kale; dusty miller and ivy will help to dress these plantings up.

WINTER: It's amazing how many greens there are. Experiment with evergreen boughs in various combinations, as well as: Evergreen boughs with dogwood branches; a row of miniature conifers; in milder climates, add sprigs of heather or berried holly for colour.

PERENNIALS

P erennials are the mainstay of the garden —
faithful plants that for the most part return
year after year. Growing easy-care, long-
flowering perennials in your garden gives you
more time to look after other gardening jobs while
still having lots of colour and interest around you.
I've chosen a group of my favourite perennials that
are reliable and quite hardy, have fairly long
blooming periods, and will add beauty to any garden. But first, here is a quick look at some tips for
choosing perennials and caring for them.

BUYING PERENNIALS

❀ The small plant you buy in a pot at the garden
centre can grow into a monster in a few short years.
Check not only its mature height but the spread.

❀ You can start perennials from seed, but most people
prefer to buy nursery-grown plants at a garden
centre or other supplier. These plants usually
already have a season's growth and you can more
easily see what the plant will look like when mature.

❀ Buy plants that are bushy and full, not leggy. Plants
should have good green leaves and preferably be in
bud. If you want to be sure of the colour, look for
those that have a flower or two open.

PLANTING PERENNIALS

❀ We are inclined to plant things closely together to make the garden look fuller. Resist this urge when planting perennials. In a very short time these plants will fill out. Use annuals to fill in bare spaces in a new perennial bed.

❀ Water the plant about an hour before you intend to plant it with diluted 5-15-5 transplanter fertilizer.

❀ Dig a hole about twice the size of the root ball and deep enough so that the soil line on the ball will be just below the top of the new hole. Dig in generous quantities of compost, bone meal, or fish meal to amend the soil.

❀ Turn potted plants on their side, tap the bottom of the pot, and pull the plant out of the container. Use your thumbs to push plants out of thin plastic six-packs. For peat pots, cut off the part of the pot that extends above the soil line and remove the bottom of the pot, leaving the sides. The pot itself will eventually decompose in the soil.

❀ Handle all potted plants with care. Don't yank or pull them too hard. Plant immediately. Gently spread the roots out. Fill the hole halfway with soil and tamp it down carefully with your fist. Continue filling and tamping until the hole has been filled to the same level as the surrounding bed. Water thoroughly.

❀ On bare-root plants, cut off any damaged roots. Gently spread the roots in the bottom of the hole. Fill halfway with soil. Tamp, fill with more soil, and continue until the hole is filled. Water.

Russian sage, or perovskia, centre, was the 1995 perennial of the year.

CARING FOR PERENNIALS

In hot and dry summers, you will have to supplement the rainfall. Infrequent deep soakings of about two hours at one time are better than frequent light waterings. Watering deeply encourages the roots to grow further into the soil, where they will find more nutrients and moisture. Shallow watering causes shallow roots, which are more susceptible to varying temperatures and rainfalls.

Every now and then give your plants a treat with a gentle spray just to spruce them up a bit. This is not meant as a watering but as a cleansing bath. This cleansing is particularly important in city gardens to remove dust and other pollutants from the plants.

Fertilize perennials in the spring with some well-rotted compost or manure. Gently work it into the soil around the roots. In May, June, and July apply a 6-12-12 fertilizer according to directions, but discontinue fertilizing after midsummer.

Mulching keeps down weeds, keeps roots cool, conserves moisture, inhibits soil heaving in winter freeze-thaw cycles, and prevents fungus spores from reaching the leaves of the plants. Mulching consists of spreading material or a mixture of materials, such as peat moss, compost, bark chips, pine needles, on top of the soil and around the plants. (See *The Complete Gardener, Planting and Growing*, page 43).

SOME USEFUL PERENNIALS

PERENNIAL CORNFLOWER   *Centaurea*
Easy to grow, drought tolerant, native

These low maintenance plants are perfect for northern climates. Grow from seed if you can't find potted plants. Cut the plant back if the leaves begin to yellow and it will produce new leaves and flowers.

COLOURS: Pink, blue, or yellow, with silvery or felted foliage
ZONE: To Zone 2, depending on variety
HEIGHT: 30 cm to 120 cm (1 to 4 feet)
LIGHT REQUIREMENTS: Full sun to light shade
BLOOMING PERIOD: Late spring and early summer
USES: Good for the dry border; informal beds; flowers can be used in fresh or dried arrangements.

SHASTA DAISY   *Chrysanthemum × superbum*
Long blooming period

I'm always happy to see the cheerful nodding heads of this great performer. Cut it back hard when blooming stops and you'll get another round of slightly smaller flowers in late summer. It likes well-drained soil but don't let the soil get too dry.

COLOURS: White petals, yellow centre
ZONE: To Zone 4
HEIGHT: 30 cm to 90 cm (1 to 3 feet)

LIGHT REQUIREMENTS: Full sun
BLOOMING PERIOD: June to August
Uses: Great companions for irises, poppies, daylilies, and yarrows. Makes good cut flowers. Clumps grow aggressively year to year.

SIBERIAN IRIS   *Iris siberica*
Prefers a moist spot, easy care

Reliable and pest-free, all they ask is a damp spot for their feet. Neat near a pond.

COLOURS: Purple, white, blue, yellow, deep red
ZONE: To Zone 2
HEIGHT: 30 cm to 90 cm (1 to 3 feet)
LIGHT REQUIREMENTS: Full sun to part shade
BLOOMING PERIOD: Late spring to early summer
USES: In beds with other spring and early summer perennials; with ferns, hostas. The long sword-like blades combine well with rounded shapes and bold flowers.

LAMB'S EARS   *Stachys byzantina*
Soft grey foliage

A member of the mint family. Likes a moist, well-drained soil. In areas with frequent rain or high humidity, rot can set in as the woolly foliage traps water. If rot has afflicted your lamb's ears, cut the plant back and it will recover in dryer and cooler weather.

COLOURS: Small pink or purple flowers, outshone by the beautiful foliage
ZONE: To Zone 4
HEIGHT: 30 cm to 45 cm (12 to 18 inches)
LIGHT REQUIREMENTS: Full sun to light shade
BLOOMING PERIOD: June and July
USES: Looks nice with irises; put at the front of the border; use as a transition plant from one colour grouping to another or as part of the white garden; makes a good ground cover.

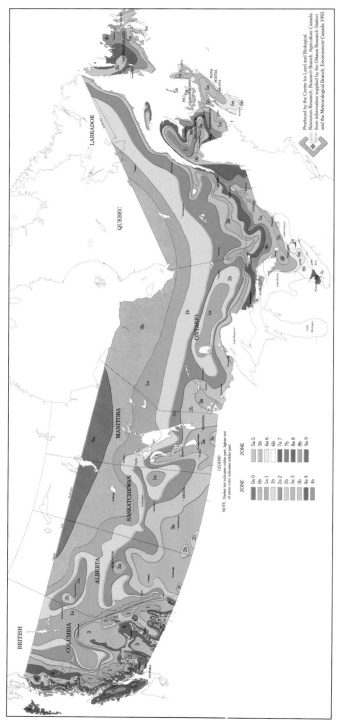

Produced by the Centre for Land and Biological Resources Research, Research Branch, Agriculture Canada from information supplied by the Ottawa Research Station and the Meteorological Branch, Environment Canada 1993.

LEGEND

NOTE: Darker tint indicates colder part, lighter tint of same color indicates milder part.

ZONE		ZONE	
0a	0	5a	5
0b		5b	
1a	1	6a	6
1b		6b	
2a	2	7a	7
2b		7b	
3a	3	8a	8
3b		8b	
4a	4	9a	9
4b			

ZONES: TEMPERATURE AND PLACES

The average annual minimum temperatures represented by the zones are shown below, together with some of the Canadian places in those zones:

❄ **ZONE 0:** − 45°C (–50°F); SK: La Loche, La Ronge; MB: Thompson

❄ **ZONE 1:** below -45°C (–50°F); SK: Prince Albert; MB: The Pas; ON: Timmins; PQ: Gagnon, Chibougamau

❄ **ZONE 2:** –45°C to –40°C (¨–50°F to –40°F); BC: Prince George; AB: Grande Prairie; SK: Regina, Saskatoon; MB: Brandon; ON: Fort Frances, Sioux Lookout; PQ: Noranda, Baie Comeau

❄ **ZONE 3:** –40°C to –34°C (–40°F to –30°F); AB: Lethbridge, Calgary, Edmonton; SK: Swift Current; MB: Portage la Prairie, Winnipeg, Dauphin; ON: Thunder Bay; NB: Edmunston

❄ **ZONE 4:** –34°C to –29°C (–30°F to –20°F); ON: Sault Ste. Marie, Sudbury; PQ: Quebec City, Trois Rivières; NB: Campbellton; NF: Gander, Corner Brook

❄ **ZONE 5:** –29°C to –23°C (–20°F to –10°F); ON: Kingston, Ottawa, Barrie; PQ: Montreal; NB: Saint John, Moncton, Fredericton; NF: St. John's

❄ **ZONE 6:** –23°C to –17°C (–10°F to 0°F); BC: Kamloops; ON: Metro Toronto, London; NS: Sydney, Yarmouth, Halifax; PE: Charlottetown

❄ **ZONE 7:** –17°C to –12°C (0°F to 10°F); BC: Trail; ON: Windsor, Chatham

❄ **ZONE 8:** –12°C to –7°C (10°F to 20°F); BC: Vancouver, Victoria

❄ **ZONE 9:** –7°C to –1°C (20°F to 30°F); BC: parts of westernmost coast.

....

DAYLILY *Hemerocallis*

Long blooming period. A Prairie garden favourite!

One of the easiest and most satisfying plants to grow. Even though each bloom lasts only a day, there is a seemingly endless supply of buds ready for tomorrow's show during the growing season. By choosing your varieties carefully, you can have daylilies in bloom from May through September.

COLOURS: Creamy white, yellow, crimson, purple, pink, orange, red, burgundy
ZONE: To Zone 1
HEIGHT: 30 cm to 165 cm (1 to 5 1/2 feet)
LIGHT REQUIREMENTS: Full sun to part shade
BLOOMING PERIOD: May through September, depending on variety
USES: In the mixed border, but especially impressive when planted in masses — on banks, along walkways, as a foundation plant. Attractive foliage maintains interest before and after flowering.

....

HOSTA *Hosta*

Made for the shade

One of the most useful plants in the shade garden. Available in a wide range of colours and textures — you are sure to find one suitable for your needs. Easy to divide in the spring. Warning: hostas like moist soil, but so do slugs. Is it any wonder that slugs like hostas?

COLOURS: Greens: greenish blue, white-edged, deep green, grey-green, yellow and green, blue-grey; flowers are white or pale purple, over 300 varieties available.
Zone: To Zone 3
HEIGHT: 15 cm to 90 cm (18 to 42 inches)
LIGHT REQUIREMENTS: Shade
BLOOMING PERIOD: Summer to fall, though not usually grown for its flowers

*Daylilies, facing page, come in a wide variety of colours.
They look especially grand planted in masses.*

USES: Plant with ferns, wildflowers, and other shade-
loving perennials, under large trees, along a shady
walk, as ground covers, in containers. Good plant to
disguise the fading foliage of spring bulbs as the
hostas emerge just as the bulbs are finishing.

GOLDEN MARGUERITE   *Anthemis tinctoria*
Easy, even in poor soil

Ferny foliage and a profusion of cheerful daisy-like
blooms make this a splendid plant. It reblooms in the fall,
so it is very useful in the mixed border. Plant might need
staking and needs deadheading to keep it blooming.

COLOURS: Yellow
ZONE: To Zone 4 (in Zone 3, it might act like a bienni-
al, completing its life cycle in two years then dying)
HEIGHT: 30 cm to 90 cm (1 to 3 feet)
LIGHT REQUIREMENTS: Sun
BLOOMING PERIOD: Early summer to early fall
USES: Looks great with blue sage, cranesbill, and bee-
balm. Try it in a container or as a filler between
other plants. Cut flowers are long-lasting.

SEDUM 'AUTUMN JOY'   *Sedum*
Attracts butterflies

Through the seasons, the flower buds change from bright green to pink, rose, then finally rust. Like yarrow, the dry flower heads will provide a lacy contrast against the winter snow. Use as a cut flower but don't put it in water — it will last indoors for weeks just as is.

COLOURS: Changes from green to deep rust
ZONE: To Zone 2
HEIGHT: 60 cm (2 feet)
LIGHT REQUIREMENTS: Full sun or light shade
BLOOMING PERIOD: Late summer
USES: In middle of border, as a low hedge, to brighten a spot in late summer and early autumn.

THRIFT   *Armeria*
For the seaside rock garden

Although this is seen in the seaside rock garden, don't confine this low-grower just to the seaside as it will do well anywhere in Canada as long as it has a sunny spot and well-drained soil.

COLOURS: White, pink, rosy red
ZONE: To Zone 2
HEIGHT: 15 cm to 30 cm (6 inches to 1 foot), depending on variety
LIGHT REQUIREMENTS: Full sun
BLOOMING PERIOD: June to September
USES: Rock gardens, wall gardens, troughs, between paving stones.

YARROW   *Achillea*
Provides winter interest

Deadheading will keep yarrow blooming but leave some late flower heads on the plant. They will become dry and brown and will look attractive against snow in the dead of winter. Plant might need staking. It grows and multiplies quite aggressively. Excellent for giving your garden a natural look.

COLOURS: White, pale and bright yellow, pink, rose, red; ferny, grey, aromatic foliage
ZONE: To Zone 2
HEIGHT: 45 cm to 90 cm (18 to 36 inches) depending on variety
LIGHT REQUIREMENTS: Full sun
BLOOMING PERIOD: Summer to late fall, depending on variety
USES: In middle or back of border. Softens bold textures and acts as foil to plants with erect stems.

YUCCA   *Yucca*
Exotic-looking but easy. Loves to be ignored in dry, poor soil

Easy to grow and provides a dramatic touch to the garden. It is tolerant of heat and drought. Herbaceous. It is not a true perennial and is usually classified as a broad-leaf evergreen.

COLOURS: Creamy white flowers, but also grown for its tall spiky leaves
ZONE: To Zone 4
HEIGHT: 2 m (7 feet)
LIGHT REQUIREMENTS: Full sun to light shade
BLOOMING PERIOD: Summer
USES: Plant alone or in combination with perennials that have soft leaves.

ROCK GARDENS

A rock garden, a popular addition to many Canadian gardens, uses plants that are fairly undemanding once they are given the conditions they like best — very well-draining soil and exposure to the sun for a good part of the day. In areas that have hot summers, site the rock garden so that it is facing east, northeast, or northwest. If this is not possible, try to provide shade for the hottest part of the day.

❋ If you have a rocky situation already, it won't take you long to create a rock garden. As much as possible, make the rock garden look like a natural part of the landscape. In fact, I think the use of rocks and water in modern gardening is taking on a Canadian landscape identity as opposed to, for example, an English or Californian landscape.

❋ A rock garden can add interest to a flat landscape.

❋ Build a rock garden as a backdrop for a water garden — it is a way of using the rocks, soil, and debris that you excavate as you dig the hole for the water garden.

❋ Rock garden plants are small, which allows you to grow more plants in a smaller area than you can in a perennial bed.

BUILDING THE ROCK GARDEN

❋ Build the rock garden on a sloping site to improve the drainage.

❋ Incorporate large rocks so that only a section of them protrudes from the soil. It might seem a waste to hide the largest part of the rock, but it will make the landscape more natural looking and provide stability. Try to make the large rocks — which should all be the same type of rock — look as if they are part of an outcropping that has always been there. Imagine how these rocks would look in their natural surroundings and duplicate that as faithfully as possible. Examine the rock to see the direction of the strata lines and line them up as you lay the rocks.

❋ In a well-designed rock garden, between one-third and one-half of it should be rock.

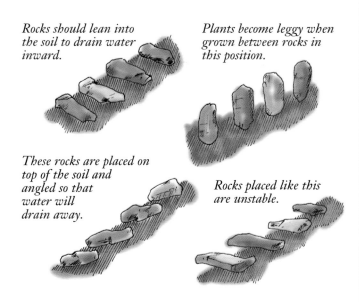

Rocks should lean into the soil to drain water inward.

Plants become leggy when grown between rocks in this position.

These rocks are placed on top of the soil and angled so that water will drain away.

Rocks placed like this are unstable.

Cross-Section Showing How to Place Rocks

Slope rocks back into the centre of the rock garden so that soil will run down the rock and be absorbed by soil around the rocks. It shouldn't run off the front of the rock.

Porous rocks (limestone is the traditional favourite) are preferred because they store moisture and keep the ground beneath them cool, which alpine plants like. Sandstone and limestone are porous; granite is not.

Hire a contractor to move and place large rocks. Your back will thank you.

The soil should be well-drained. This is not a place that you have to build up with compost and well-rotted manure, although you can lay a base of good garden soil over which you put the planting mixture of loam, peat moss, and grit (coarser than sand).

Mound soil over and between the rocks as you place the rocks, making sure air pockets are filled. During the first year, the soil will settle, so be generous.

✳ Keep very small pebbles, stones, and gravel to use as a top dressing or mulch once the plantings are complete. Try to match the colour of the stones used as mulch to the colour of the stones used for the main boulders in the rock garden. The stone mulch should be about 3.75 cm to 5 cm (1.5 to 2 inches) deep.

✳ Once the rock garden is assembled, with the mulch set aside to add after plantings are done, it is time for the real fun of choosing the plants.

✳ If you don't have the space for a rock garden, nearly all the plants used in rock gardening can be planted in stone troughs.

PLANTING AND CARE TIPS

✳ Position alpines so their roots can touch rock — their natural habitat.

✳ Use permanent plant labels for each plant. When the plants are young, it can be hard to tell them

Daffodils and hyacinth are lovely in the rock garden.

apart. In a few years, when they have matured, you will probably know them all by name and by sight but your visitors may be interested in reading their name tags.

Water with 5-15-5 transplanting fertilizer and then plant. Water again. Unless the weather is overcast, keep new plants shaded for the first week, if possible.

PLANTS FOR ROCK GARDENS

When you are choosing plants for the rock garden, don't forget dwarf shrubs and conifers; the smaller bulbs such as crocus and anemones; and annuals such as lobelia, nasturtium, portulaca, and alyssum. There are hundreds of interesting and unusual plants for the rock garden — join your local garden society devoted to rock gardening to find out more about this fascinating specialty.

RULE OF THUMB:

Rock gardens, without exception, are for people who have a passion for gardening. If you don't, the hand weeding will overcome any enthusiasm you may have for the idea. Minimize weeding by applying a granular pre-emergent weed preventor in early spring.

ADONIS: Perennial; buttercup-like yellow flowers open in early to mid spring; ferny foliage; plant in sun or part shade; needs well-drained but moisture-retentive soil; height to 20 cm to 30 cm (8 to 12 inches), spread 30 cm (12 inches); Zone 3

AUBRETIA (Purple rock cress): Perennial; forms mats; flowers are blue, red, purple, or pink; blooms in mid spring to early summer; cut back when flowers have faded; Zone 4

❋ **Rock cress** (*Arabis*): Perennial; white flowers; soft grey foliage; grow in full sun in well-drained soil; height to 15 cm (6 inches) or less, depending on variety, spread 60 cm (2 feet); Zone 3

❋ **Rock soapwort** (*Saponaria*): Perennial; trailing sprays of small pink flowers; blooms in late spring; sun; well-drained soil; cut back after flowering; height 7.5 cm (3 inches), spread 15 cm to 30 cm (6 to 12 inches); Zone 3

❋ **Saxifrage:** Perennial; another large group of plants; forms creeping cushions or rosettes; foliage silver or variegated, flowers white, purple, pink, yellow; heights and spreads vary with variety, but heights start at 10 cm (4 inches) and go to 60 cm (2 feet); blooms late spring to early summer; sun or partial shade; Zone 6

❋ **Sedum:** Perennial; encompasses a large group of plants; look for the low-growing varieties (7.5 cm/3 inches); can have eventual spread of 60 cm (2 feet); great range of colours in both foliage and flowers; full sun to partial shade; easy to grow; Zone 3

❋ **Speedwell** (*Veronica prostrata*): Perennial; deep blue flowers in early summer; sun or partial shade; height 7.5 cm (3 inches), spread 90 cm (3 feet); Zone 5

❋ **Thyme:** Perennial, though can be short-lived; many varieties grown for their scented creeping foliage; pink-purple flowers; height 2.5 cm to 7.5 cm (1 to 3 inches), spread to 60 cm (2 feet); Zone 4

BULBS, CORMS, RHIZOMES, AND TUBERS

O ne thing I like about gardening and sharing information with other gardeners is the sense of optimism we all seem to have. Gardens are never really finished and this is never more true than in the fall. Plans abound for what we'll do in the future and we look forward to seeing how newly planted perennials, shrubs, and vines will flourish next year. We also know that without some planning and planting in the fall, we will have a dreary spring and a long wait for the first blossoms. That is where spring bulbs come in.

Fall is the time to buy and plant spring-flowering bulbs — buried treasures that yield their reward just when we need it. With a bit of planning, you can have a succession of colour from March (earlier on the milder west coast) to June, just from bulbs.

In addition to the spring-flowering bulbs, in this chapter we will have a look at some summer-flowering bulbs as well as corms, rhizomes, and tubers. Corms, rhizomes, and tubers are sometimes

Hyacinth is a spring bulb that blooms after daffodils and before tulips appear.

referred to as bulbs, and, in fact, they do have something in common: they are all food storage units for the plant.

* Corms die after blooming but produce new corms for next year's growth. Some corms are dog-tooth violet, acidanthera, freesia, and gladiolus. Crocuses are actually corms, but since they are traditionally included in lists of spring bulbs, I'm going along with that convention.

* Rhizomes include daylilies, bearded irises, lily of the valley, and cannas.

* Tubers are not winter-hardy so they need to be lifted and stored each fall, a feature that takes them out of the low-maintenance category. However, many beautiful flowers grow from tubers — the popular dahlia is one — and since they make perfect container plants, I'll give you a quick rundown of some of my favourite tubers and their care.

SPRING-FLOWERING BULBS

The following popular spring bulbs are listed in the sequence in which they usually bloom. Naturally, in colder zones the blooming will start later than in milder zones, but the sequence will be the same. Bulbs can be made to bloom earlier by planting them on the south side of your home against a rock which is warmed by the spring sun and radiates the heat into the evening.

- Snowdrops
- Crocus
- Reticulata iris
- Glory-of-the-snow
- Scilla
- Grape hyacinth
- Early tulips, species tulips
- Species and miniature daffodils
- Standard daffodils
- Hyacinth
- Crown Imperial
- Tulips, tall varieties
- Allium

BUYING BULBS

The bulbs should come from a reliable source.

They should be firm and plump and free of soft spots or bruises — like a healthy onion.

Bulbs bought in bulk could save you some money.

PLANTING BULBS

If you can't plant your bulbs right away, spread them out in a cool airy place, such as your garage, until you can get them planted.

✽ Don't leave them in the bags for more than a couple of weeks.

✽ Plant early-flowering bulbs, such as crocus, aconite, snowdrops and all daffodils, in the early fall; hyacinths can be planted in midfall, and tulips can be put in any time until freeze-up.

✽ Bulbs look best planted in drifts (clumps) — imagine the outline of a large teardrop or a spiral and plant within that shape. I like to naturalize small bulbs in the lawn by tossing a handful of bulbs over my shoulder and letting them land in a random fashion. I plant them where they land.

✽ Plant early-flowering bulbs where you will be able to see them from the house — but not too far away as they often are small.

✽ Plant bulbs in drifts or clumps of one kind and one colour for a better splash of colour.

✽ Prepare the bed by digging it well, removing weeds and stones. It is important that the soil be well-drained or the bulbs will rot in the ground. Add organic material, ideally from your compost.

✽ Dig a hole for each individual bulb or make a wider hole to take a grouping. The depth of the hole is dictated by the diameter of the bulb — the depth of the hole should be a little more than twice the diameter of the bulb.

✽ Plant your bulbs in layers if those bulbs are to bloom in sequence. For example, you might plant tulip bulbs that bloom in May in a hole, partially fill in the hole, then plant some snowdrops, which will bloom in March, in the same hole.

✽ Sprinkle a handful of bulb food or bone meal in the planting hole before planting and scratch it in with your fingers.

Tulips just can't be beat for bringing vibrant colour to the spring garden.

❄ Put the bulb in the hole, pointed end up, and give it a little twist to engage it firmly with the soil. Space the bulbs about 2.5 cm (1 inch) apart. Don't let the bulbs touch one another.

❄ Sprinkle the bulbs with bulb dust, which you can obtain at garden centres, to protect them from insects and disease.

❄ Cover them with soil, then firm the soil in place with your heel.

❄ Add a healthy layer of mulch for insulation, then water well — to a depth of 5 cm to 7.5 cm (2 to 3 inches).

❄ Label the plantings or keep a small diagram to remind yourself where you have planted the bulbs.

FOILING SQUIRRELS

❄ Plant bulbs deeply — at least 10 cm (4 inches).

❄ Plant Crown Imperial near other bulbs — squirrels and moles dislike its odour.

❁ Sprinkle blood meal over the planted area and water. The blood meal needs to be damp to make it effective in repelling squirrels. It will need to be renewed after rains.

❁ Cayenne pepper or commercial rodent repellent sprinkled on the planted area repels squirrels and other animals.

❁ Cover the planted area with chicken wire.

RULE OF THUMB:

Cutting up cheap daffodil bulbs and sprinkling the finely chopped bulbs over the planted tulips is an effective way of keeping squirrels out of the bulb bed. A CTV viewer from Montreal taught me this trick. Squirrels hate daffodil bulbs because they are bitter.

Allium, also known as Flowering Onion, is a striking addition to the spring border.

CARING FOR BULBS

❄ Pick off the dead flowers, but leave the foliage even though it looks untidy. This is very important as the foliage helps build energy in the bulb. Once the foliage is quite yellow, remove it with a gentle tug. If it resists, leave it for a few more days then cut it off.

❄ Feed the bulbs with a 6-12-12 fertilizer after flowering.

❄ Water the bulbs during dry spells.

❄ Dig the bulbs up in September and divide them if bulbs produce fewer and fewer flowers every year. You will probably find that they have produced bulblets. Replant the bulblets; many will flower next spring, but it may take some a couple of years to produce.

SOME SUGGESTED SPRING BULBS

ALLIUM (Flowering Onion)

COLOURS: Rose, purple, white
HEIGHT: Spring-flowering varieties — up to 90 cm (36 inches)
GROWING CONDITIONS: Sunny spot in fertile, well-drained loam.
COMMENTS: Kids just love the look of this one. A versatile addition to the border. For the spring border, be sure you get the varieties that bloom in the spring. Other members of this family bloom in summer and fall. The late spring-blooming tall varieties add vertical interest. Plant them with bushy plants that will hide their foliage as it turns yellow.

CROCUS

COLOURS: Yellow, cream, white, purple, blue
HEIGHT: 10 cm to 15 cm (4 to 6 inches)

GROWING CONDITIONS: Likes a sunny protected spot. Prefers a light soil to a heavy boggy soil.

COMMENTS: Plant 10 cm (4 inches) deep any time from August to October. Species crocus (sometimes called small-flowered crocus) bloom early and stand up well to stormy weather; hybrid (large-flowered crocus) bloom a bit later. Plant in groups for the best display. Good in rock gardens; naturalized in the lawn; with other bulbs or wildflowers.

CROWN IMPERIAL

COLOURS: Bell-like flowers in bright orange, red, yellow

HEIGHT: Height: 120 cm (4 feet)

GROWING CONDITIONS: Sun or light shade; well-drained spot with light rich soil.

COMMENTS: Makes a bold statement in the garden; position it carefully. Combine it with dwarf flowering shrubs and foliage perennials.

DAFFODIL

COLOURS: Red gold to yellow to pale cream

HEIGHT: Species, 10 cm to 15 cm (4 to 6 inches); hybrids, 15 cm to 60 cm (6 to 24 inches)

GROWING CONDITIONS: Likes a cool spot in sun or partial shade and a well-drained loamy soil.

COMMENTS: Hybrids: Plant among perennials that will grow up and around the yellowing foliage, which must be left to ripen. Species or miniature: Use in a rock garden.

RULE OF THUMB:

Daffodils offer the best value for the money, in my books. They grow and multiply over a five- to eight-year period at which time they need digging up and replanting. They bloom early, many are fragrant, and they are great as cut flowers — plus, I love their peculiar look!

GLORY-OF-THE-SNOW

COLOURS: Star-shaped violet to blue flowers
HEIGHT: 10 cm to 15 cm (4 to 6 inches)
GROWING CONDITIONS: Tolerant of most soils. Sunny
spot or part shade.
COMMENTS: Looks good growing in the lawn. If you
leave the grass-like foliage uncut, the plant will naturalize itself. Also nice under trees and shrubs where
they form a lovely blue sweep if left undisturbed.

GRAPE HYACINTH

COLOURS: Purple, white
HEIGHT: 18 cm to 20 cm (6 to 8 inches)
GROWING CONDITIONS: Tolerant of many soils.
Prefers sun.
COMMENTS: Very easy to grow. Another great natural-
izer — best planted where it can multiply to its
heart's content.

HYACINTH

COLOURS: Blue, white, pink, pale yellow
HEIGHT: 20 cm to 30 cm (8 to 12 inches)
GROWING CONDITIONS: Plant in a well-drained sunny
spot.
COMMENTS: Many are fragrant. Not easy to grow
in regions with severe winters; gardeners in the
north and on the prairies can reserve them for winter forcing.

RETICULATA IRIS

COLOURS: Purple with yellow markings
HEIGHT: 20 cm to 30 cm (8 to 12 inches)
GROWING CONDITIONS: Sunny spot. Prefers a well-
drained sandy loam.
COMMENTS: Also called netted iris and bulbous iris.
May not bloom every year so plant some every year.

PLANTS

SCILLA

COLOURS: Bright blue
HEIGHT: 10 cm to 15 cm (4 to 6 inches)
GROWING CONDITIONS: Full sun or partial shade.
COMMENTS: Prolific spreader will provide a beautiful blue spring carpet in a few years and will thrive for many more years!

SNOWDROPS

COLOURS: White
HEIGHT: 10 cm (4 inches)
GROWING CONDITIONS: If possible, plant where they will be protected from afternoon sun to extend blooming time. Loamy soil.
COMMENTS: Plant by mid-September. Will increase if left in place. Blooms appear in late winter and can last for several weeks; because they bloom early, plant where you will be able to see them from the house or near a well-used walkway.

TULIPS

COLOURS: Nearly any colour you could want (except black or blue): white, pink, every shade of red, orange, purple, yellow, golden yellow, green yellow....
HEIGHT: 15 cm to 90 cm (6 to 36 inches)
GROWING CONDITIONS: Put in a sunny spot in well-drained soil.
COMMENTS: Can be planted until the ground freezes. The species tulips are good in a rock garden or at the front of a border. Tulips are divided into early, mid, and late blooming. Take note of the type you are buying.

RULE OF THUMB

Tulips grow and flower without fail almost everywhere in Canada, regardless of winter severity — unless the squirrels eat them first! (See the Rule of Thumb on page 44.) So, if you are looking for a way of getting your kids or grandchildren involved in gardening, hand them some tulips and help them to plant the bulbs in a prominent place. The kids will be really excited when the tulips start poking through the ground in the spring.

SUMMER-FLOWERING BULBS, CORMS, RHIZOMES, AND TUBERS

Some of the summer-flowering bulbs and corms need to be stored indoors in winter in a cool dry spot, but certain ones can also be grown in and spend their winters in containers in a cool dry spot. Here are some favourites.

AUTUMN CROCUS OR COLCHICUM (not a real crocus!): Corm with pink, white, violet, or lilac flowers that appear in the fall. A question I am often asked on my

The beautiful Thunderbolt Lily is just one member of the huge lily family.

radio show is about the strange bulb-like plant that produces leaves but no flowers in the spring — well, that's colchicum! Best planted in amongst a low ground cover; height 45 cm to 60 cm (18 to 24 inches); full sun and well-drained, fertile soil. To Zone 5.

DAHLIAS: Easy-to-grow tuber; great variety of colours — white, yellow, pink, purple, red, orange, maroon; rich soil; full or partial sun; keep well watered when they start blooming in late summer; deadhead frequently. Winter storage: dig up after the first light frost, knock off soil, let dry in sun. Dust with sulphur; store in cool dry room in a box or paper bag of vermiculite (never plastic!), peat moss, sawdust, or sand; keep at 2°C to 10°C (35°F to 50°F). Check occasionally; if they start to shrivel, add a little water; if they have some growth, open the container to let some of the moisture evaporate. Divide them in the spring when bud growth starts.

GLADIOLUS: Corm that needs rich, well-drained soil in the full sun. Plant in one-week intervals beginning about two weeks before the last frost and ending in mid June (4 to 6 plantings). Fertilize with 6-12-12, and keep well watered. Ruffled blooms come in a wide range of colours, start in late July, continue for about two weeks. May need staking; can grow to 1.5 m (5 feet). Winter storage: When leaves turn brown, dig up corms, remove foliage. Harvest new corms, discard old. Let new corms dry in a shady spot until the soil flakes off, then treat with bulb dust before storing in mesh bags in a cool — 2°C to 7°C (35°F to 45°F) — dry, dark place. Plant in different location next year.

BEARDED IRIS: Rhizome with fan of broad leaves; outstanding flowers for the early summer border in shades of purple, yellow, blue; height 60 cm to 90 cm (2 to 3 feet); likes sunny spot in average garden soil as long as it's not too acid. When planting, top of rhizome should be just visible above the soil; keep well watered until established.

Iris, such as this germanica species, are valuable in the garden for both their flowers and the shape of their leaves.

❀ **LILIES:** Choose varieties carefully for stunning bloom from June through summer. Best at back of the border. Plant bulbs in well-drained soil; can stay in ground over winter, but mulch for the first few years. Prefer full sun but tolerate some shade. It takes a season to build up their roots, but once they have settled in, they will last for years, providing beauty and scent in your garden. Divide them every few years if they seem less productive.

WATER GARDENS

Some of the easiest plants to care for are those for the water garden. Not only are they among the most beautiful plants, but they offer great variety in height, colour, and texture. You don't even need a full-fledged water garden, either, to grow some of these plants. Try water gardening in a container on a patio or balcony; make a bog garden; or put a boggy area of your garden to work.

❀ Design your water garden so that it has several levels. That way you can grow marginal plants — those that just like to get their feet wet — as well as those that need depth, such as water lilies. If you have one depth and it's over 45 cm (18 inches) deep, use bricks to make ledges to set marginal plants on.

To cut down on algae in both the water garden and container water garden, keep the surface partially shaded with the leaves of plants, but to no more than 70% of the total area. Use plants called oxygenators — these are plants that compete with algae for carbon dioxide, which they absorb from the water; in the process, they release oxygen, essential for life in the water garden.

Container water gardens can be partially sunk in the ground rather than sitting on a deck. Use any non-porous container — just be sure it has a good wide mouth. The style you choose should blend with the overall design of the garden. For example, a wooden half-barrel fits right in in an informal garden.

The plantings in containers should be in keeping with the size of the container.

A water garden can be constructed in a container such as a barrel. This is a good way to try out this kind of gardening before committing to a full-scale version.

PLANTS FOR THE WATER GARDEN

❀ Water garden plants are usually contained individually in pots since many have aggressive roots that would eventually crowd out less vigorous plants.

❀ Water lilies are the most popular plant for the water garden. They are beautiful and easy to look after. Although conventional wisdom has it that they need at least six hours of sun daily to bloom, some of the hardy ones will bloom with less.

❀ **HARDY WATER LILIES:** They need about 45 cm (18 inches) of water to grow properly. They are not as showy as tropical water lilies, but they can stay in the pool over the winter with very little maintenance. Colours are white, pink, red, yellow, peach, or red in a variety of blossom shapes — like cups, stars, or double peonies. They have a light scent. Blossoms will last three or four days, closing at night. To prepare hardy water lilies for winter, cut off all foliage and move the plant to the deepest part of the pool to prevent their roots from freezing. Most hardy varieties can be grown to Zone 4.

❀ **TROPICAL WATER LILIES:** They bloom profusely, sending their blossoms high above the water. The flowers are white, pink, peach, red, yellow, purple, and blue; are quite fragrant, and can be star-shaped or cup-shaped. The blossoms last for three to five days. Night-blooming tropicals are usually heavily scented. Tropicals need to be lifted in the fall. Cut back all foliage and place the plant in a black garbage bag. Store it in a cool spot, free of frost, over the winter. A cool basement room is ideal.

❀ **WATER LETTUCE:** A floating tropical that should be treated as an annual in Canada; sends out runners from the parent over the growing season, greatly increasing the coverage; leaves are grey-green, felted, erect, and shell-shaped; mature plants are about 15 cm (6 inches) across.

(left) A hardy water lily can stay in the water garden over winter. The tropical water lily (right) must be stored in a cool, frost-free location during winter.

VAILLISNERIA: Also called tape grass or ribbon grass; ribbon-like pale green leaves; filters water and provides shelter and food for fish; water depth 15 cm to 60 cm (6 to 24 inches); submerged floater, but planted in pot it has a good chance of over-wintering to Zone 4.

DUCKWEED: A bright green floating plant; good fish food. This one is a rapid spreader so keep an eye out!

WATER HYACINTH: Another floating tropical that self-propagates over the summer; trailing roots help shade the water and offer protection for small fish; foliage is shiny green with swollen pods at the base; produces attractive pale lavender flowers; excellent water purifier, slowing algae growth; prefers full sun.

WATER THYME: A submerged floating oxygenator; treat as annual; its leaves provide good protection for fish and their spawn; minimum depth of water: 15 cm (6 inches)

HERB GARDENS

I always enjoy having fresh sprigs of parsley, basil, or thyme to add to my favourite dishes. Growing herbs in pots, either indoors or on the patio or balcony, is one way to ensure a steady supply of these aromatic and useful plants. But if you have the space, a section of the garden can be set aside for a herb garden — or use a small front garden in which to plant a decorative herb garden in the form of the traditional knot garden.

Herbs need sun and prefer fertile well-draining soil, although some will tolerate partial shade and poor soil. These are plants that have survived under harsh conditions (most are native to the Mediterranean region), but that is no reason to treat them badly in your garden!

Herb gardens traditionally have been located near the kitchen and often were planted in fairly formal and intricate patterns. By using the contrasting textures and colours of these leafy plants, you can make an attractive and practical garden.

RULE OF THUMB:

Most popular herbs are terrific low-maintenance plants because they originated in the Mediterranean region. They enjoy a period of dryness between watering, are tolerant of less than ideal soil conditions, and demand little in the way of fertilizer — though I apply 20-20-20 monthly, spring through summer.

PLANTS FOR HERB GARDENS

In the following list of plants, take special note of the spread.

PLANTS

❀
BASIL: Annual. Height 30 cm to 60 cm (1 to 2 feet), spread 30 cm (1 foot). Shiny green leaves, 2.5 cm to 5 cm (1 to 2 inches) long; white or purple flowers in late summer; a smaller variety has purple leaves. Leaves have a spicy, pungent flavour.

❀
BAY: Tender perennial. Bring indoors in winter. Left unchecked, it can grow to a full-sized tree! Responds well to clipping and shaping. Dark green, glossy foliage. Use whole leaves.

❀
CHIVES: Perennial. Height 15 cm to 25 cm (6 to 10 inches), spread 30 cm (12 inches). Green grass-like foliage; lavender heads similar to clover appear in mid to late summer. Leaves have mild onion flavour.

❀
DILL: Annual. Height 60 cm to 90 cm (2 to 3 feet), spread 22 cm to 30 cm (9 to 12 inches). Green plumy foliage, blue-green stems, yellow umbrella-like flower heads. Attracts monarch butterflies.

❀
SWEET MARJORAM: Annual. Height 60 cm (2 feet), spread 30 cm to 45 cm (12 to 18 inches). Small oval grey-green leaves.

❀
MINT: Perennial. Likes a rich moist, well-drained soil; can become invasive. Height 60 cm to 90 cm (2 to 3 feet), spread 30 cm to 45 cm (12 to 18 inches). Green slightly textured leaves in a variety of scents, such as apple mint, spearmint, and peppermint.

❀
OREGANO: Perennial similar to sweet marjoram but shrubbier. Height 60 cm (2 feet), spread 45 cm to 60 cm (18 to 24 inches). Dark green leaves with sharper fragrance and taste than marjoram. Pinch back small white, pink, or purple flowers.

❀
PARSLEY: Grow as annual. Height 30 cm (1 foot), spread 30 cm (1 foot). Bright green, crinkly leaves with compact growth.

ROSEMARY: Tender perennial. Where ground freezes, bring indoors in winter. Height 90 cm to 180 cm (2 to 6 feet), spread 90 cm to 180 cm (2 to 6 feet). Grey-green needle-like leaves with pine scent.

SAGE: Perennial. Height 90 cm (2 feet), spread 45 cm (18 inches). Grey-green soft leaves with strong aromatic scent; purple flowers late in season.

SUMMER SAVORY: Annual. Height 30 cm to 45 cm (12 to 18 inches), spread 15 cm to 30 cm (6 to 12 inches). Small shiny green leaves, tiny lavender or pink-white flowers in midsummer; attractive to bees.

WINTER SAVORY: Perennial. Height 15 cm to 30 cm (6 to 12 inches), spread 30 cm to 45 cm (12 to 18 inches). Glossy dark leaves stiffer than summer savory, less aromatic, flowers larger. Makes good low hedge or border, especially the dwarf form.

FRENCH TARRAGON: Tender perennial. Height 60 cm (2 feet), spread 35 cm (15 inches). Use leaves, fresh or dried.

THYME: Perennial. Height 20 cm (8 inches), spread 22 cm to 30 cm (9 to 12 inches). Shrubby, low-growing, aromatic grey-green foliage, small lilac-coloured flowers; attracts bees. Makes good edging plant.

RULE OF THUMB:

Herbs are great container plants. Mary and I keep a strawberry planter full of herbs just outside our kitchen door. I recommend these favourites for planting in a container: thyme, (choose 2 or 3 from dozens available!), rosemary, basil, sweet marjoram, chives, sage.

SHRUBS AND TREES

· ·

E ven in the smallest gardens, there is room for a small shrub or tree. The vast array of shrubs and trees can at first seem overwhelming but once you narrow down what you want — and, more importantly, what you have room for — you will find it easier to reach a decision.

Are you looking for a shrub or tree with seasonal interest, such as a flowering crab for spring colour, a sumac for vibrant fall crimson, a mountain ash that produces clusters of bright orange berries in the fall, a rose bush as the centrepiece of the garden in June? Do you want quick shade? Is attracting birds important to you? Before long, you will be narrowing down your choices.

In this chapter, I will give you a sampling of the wide variety of shrubs and trees available to get you started in your search.

BUYING SHRUBS AND TREES

As with other plants, be sure the shrub or tree is hardy in your area.

Bridal Wreath Spirea is a lovely flowering shrub, with its arching sprays of delicate flowers.

❋ Check the mature height and spread. That tiny blue spruce by your front door will, in a few short years, cut out all light from entering the house and will have you feeling as if you are fighting your way through a jungle every time you go in and out.

❋ Choose healthy-looking plants with no obvious signs of disease. Most reliable garden centres and nurseries give a guarantee with shrubs and trees.

PLANTING SHRUBS AND TREES

❋ If you have ordered plants by mail, you will probably receive bare-roots plants. If you can't plant them right away, heel them in in a protected part of the

Mock orange is a shrub to plant close to the house so you can enjoy its beautiful flowers and sweet scent.

garden. To heel in, simply dig a shallow hole and lay the plant on the surface of the bed so that the roots are in the shallow hole; then cover the roots with the soil from the hole. Water in and continue to water until you are ready to plant. If you have purchased a container-grown plant and can't get it in the soil right away, keep the new plant out of the sun and water it well.

❋ Choose a site that won't interfere with overhead wires or block a desirable view.

❋ Shrubs and trees can be planted in early spring or early fall. If they are grown in containers, you can plant relatively risk free through the heat of the summer. Large trees should be moved and planted by professionals.

❋ Dig the hole at least 45 cm (18 inches) deeper than the root mass of the plant. Loosen the bottom of the soil with a fork. If the soil is heavy, loosen the sides of the hole with the fork. Mix some well-rotted compost or composted cattle manure in equal portions with the soil taken from the hole and set aside.

❁ Cut off dead stumps of wood on the new plant and
check the roots for breakages; trim off any dead or
broken roots.

❁ Insert the plant into the hole, lining up the old soil
mark so that it is level with the surface of the surrounding soil.

❁ Start to fill the hole with the topsoil you set aside. Shake
the plant every now and then to get rid of air pockets.
Continue filling, firming the soil forcefully with the ball
of your foot as you go. If the plant is a tree, insert a
stake to provide support as it establishes itself.

❁ Level the topsoil with a fork. Water sufficiently well
to reach the root zone and let drain.

CARING FOR SHRUBS AND TREES

❁ Mulch the freshly planted area with finely ground
up bark mulch. Replenish the mulch as it decompos-
es over the years.

❁ Nearly every shrub and tree benefits from pruning at
some time. Pruning brings light and air to the interi-
or of the plant, opening it up so that it will grow better and maintain its health. It also makes fruiting and
flowering shrubs and trees more productive.

❁ During prolonged periods of drought, water shrubs
and trees deeply by trickling water from the end of
the garden hose for up to two hours.

SHRUBS

All shrubs listed here will grow in full sun to light
shade and in average garden soil unless otherwise
noted.

BUTTERFLY BUSH   *Buddleia*
Attracts butterflies (it really does!)

In our garden centre, when it is full of thousands of different plants, the butterflies still find the buddleia.

COLOUR: Purple, burgundy, pink, blue, or white
ZONE: To Zone 5
HEIGHT: 1.2 m to 4.5 m (4 to 15 feet), spread 1.8 m (6 feet)
BLOOMING PERIOD: Late summer to late fall
CULTIVATION NOTES: Cut back previous year's wood in early spring. Prune again in mid spring to get large flowers. Can sometimes be slow to start growing in spring.
USES: Grey-green slender leaves make a nice contrast against dark background; butterflies are attracted to its fragrant flowers.

COTONEASTER *Cotoneaster Acutifolia* (Shrub type)
Red berries in winter

COLOUR: Pink, white; fruit is red or black
ZONE: To Zone 3, depending on variety
HEIGHT: Hedge types to 3 m (10 feet) and similar spread
BLOOMING PERIOD: Spring, followed by berries
USES: As hedge, foundation planting, in borders. Attracts cedar waxwings, blue jays, and others.

FORSYTHIA   *Forsythia*
Bright spring colour

COLOUR: Yellow
ZONE: To Zone 4
HEIGHT: 1.5 m to 2.7 m (5 to 9 feet), spread 2.5 m to 3 m (8 to 10 feet)
BLOOMING PERIOD: March to April, depending on zone
USES: Looks lovely with spring bulbs, such as grape hyacinths, planted underneath; after blooming, it is a strong leafy shrub with relatively few insect and disease problems.

Climbing Hydrangea is perfect for the shade and its flowers can easily be dried for use in floral arrangements.

....

HONEYSUCKLE   *Lonicera tataria*
Fragrant blooms, followed by berries

COLOUR: White, yellow, green-yellow, pink, red
ZONE: To Zone 2, depending on variety
HEIGHT: 1.2 m to 3 m (4 to 10 feet), 2.5 m to 3.5 m (8 to 12 feet)
BLOOMING PERIOD: Spring
USES: Many uses, since honeysuckle comes in a variety of forms: shrub, climbing, dwarf; use as hedging material, as foundation plantings, or alone. In recent years, honeysuckle in Ontario and Quebec has become prone to aphid damage.

....

HYDRANGEA   *Hydrangea*
Perfect for the shade

COLOUR: White, creamy white, pink, purple-pink
ZONE: To Zone 3, depending on variety
HEIGHT: Varies considerably — climbing hydrangea can go to 24 m (80 feet) up a wall, but the popular shrub Peegee hydrangea is a reasonable 1.5 m to 2.5 m (5 to 8 feet) in height and spread
BLOOMING PERIOD: Early summer to early fall, depending on variety
USES: Great in shady areas; climbing hydrangea makes a beautiful cover for a wall or fence with its deep green glossy leaves and scented lacy flower heads.

ROSES

For many gardeners, a garden isn't complete without a rose. Even if your garden consists of containers on a balcony, you can have a rose. Entering the kingdom of roses can be a bit daunting — what do all those names mean? Here is a brief introduction to some of the "family" names you will come across with their characteristics:

HYBRID TEA: Bushy; single or double flowers; one flower per stem; usually fragrant; great variety of colours; grow to 1 m (3 feet) or higher in milder climates; generally considered best for cutting; flower intermittently from late spring through late fall; need good winter protection in most parts of the country (to Zone 6).

FLORIBUNDA: Bushy; flowers grow in clusters; continuous flowering; less demanding to grow than hybrid teas; can be used for a low hedge; excellent roses for colour viewed from a distance; terrific bedding roses for mass plantings where a drift of colour is desired.

GRANDIFLORA: Taller than hybrid teas; flowers similar to hybrid tea but more plentiful; often blooms are born in clusters; the world's most popular rose, the

Roses with a pergola are an ideal match for a romantic garden.

Queen Elizabeth, is a grandiflora; considered excellent background roses due to their strong growth
habits; need winter protection.

❄ **TREE OR STANDARD:** Hybrid tea or floribunda, or
miniature rose grafted on to a single long (1 m/3
foot) upright stem; gorgeous focal point in a formal
garden; need good winter protection in most parts
of the country.

❄ **SHRUB:** Less showy flowers than other roses; some
are fragrant; can be put in border with other plants;
can grow 120 cm to 150 cm (4 to 5 feet) high; bloom
on old wood; very hardy.

❄ **CLIMBER AND RAMBLER:** Quite hardy; many are repeat
or ever-blooming; climbers grow up; ramblers grow
sideways or down and can be used as ground cover. See
Chapter 6 *Vines and Climbers* for more information.

❄ **MINIATURE:** 25 cm to 37 cm (10 to 15 inches) tall;
small double or semi-double flowers; excellent for
growing in containers and over-wintering indoors
under lights. They are surprisingly hardy.

RULE OF THUMB:

Look for the All Canadian Explorer Series — named
after famous Canadian explorers like Frobisher,
Cabot, McKenzie — if you are looking for a completely
winter-hardy rose that blooms beautifully in June and
July and reblooms later in the season. Growth habits
vary from 35 cm (14 inches), to 180 cm (6 feet).
Colours vary also.

With over 30,000 roses to choose from, it
would be difficult and, perhaps, misleading for me
to select just a few for inclusion in this book. If
you are planning a rose garden, or want to add
some roses to your garden, I suggest you talk to a
professional at your local garden centre.

WINTER CARE FOR ROSES

Give your roses winter protection, even in the mild zones. Most damage is done by freezing and thawing cycles, which hit us all across the country, no matter the zone we live in. Mulching is a good start and adequate for the B.C. lower mainland, but you can go to greater lengths as well.

❄ Start by mounding soil around the bush, no matter the type, to a depth of about 30 cm (12 inches). The soil can be from another part of your garden (if it's loose and rich), top soil, or triple mix (a mixture of compost, loam, and peat).

❄ Rose collars are used to contain insulating material — such as dried leaves, shredded bark, top soil, or crumpled newspapers — but have no insulating value in themselves. They help to mound the soil as high as possible up the rose canes. Don't be afraid to be generous with the newspapers — they won't hurt the roses. Any soil that remains in the spring can be spread around the bush as a mulch. Alternatives to rose collars are cages that you can build with garden netting or fine-mesh chicken wire.

RULE OF THUMB:

Roses are not high maintenance plants. They have a reputation (undeserved) for demanding a lot of your attention. This is not true if you:
- choose disease (black spot!) and insect resistant varieties (the label will tell you);
- space 75 cm (30 inches) apart — measuring centre to centre;
- plant in a sunny location (min. 6 hours per day)
- plant in an open, well-ventilated area where "gentle breezes blow";
- water throughly and never more than once a week — at night.

❄ Don't forget that snow is a good insulator. In the winter, mound extra snow over the roses to keep the ambient temperature constant.

❄ Prune roses in the spring, unless they are over 120 cm (4 feet) tall and risk being blown over. The mature canes encourage snow to accumulate around the base of the plant.

TREES

Choosing a tree for a small urban garden can be a challenge. Trees have a habit of growing a lot bigger than you ever expect — sort of like kids! But gardeners have much more control over how big their trees will grow than parents do in choosing their kids' size. When you choose a tree, you are thinking not only of this season's growth but also its future size. Here are some things to consider when choosing a tree:

- How much space do you have available?
- How much space does the tree require when fully grown?
- How fast will it grow (remember, faster can often mean messier and bigger!)?
- Do you want a fruiting or non-fruiting tree?
- Will the tree be used for a child's swing, or for shade to eat and entertain under?
- Is the purpose of the tree to block an unsightly view, or to cut down on such things as noise or soil erosion?
- Will you want a swimming pool one day?
- Will aggressive roots cause a problem with a nearby veggie garden or something else?

> ## Rule of Thumb:
> Consult with a professional when selecting a tree. A tree is an important and long-term addition to your garden. I suggest that you list the characteristics you are looking for in a tree, make a sketch of your garden and where you think you would like to locate the tree, then visit your local garden centre and talk to a professional.

SHADE GARDENS

Shade seems to be one of the biggest problems a gardener has to contend with — but in my view, it's not a problem. A challenge, yes, but not insurmountable. For example, if your shade is cast mainly by trees, plant spring bulbs under them for a bright show in early spring.

I've introduced you to some shade-tolerant and shade-loving plants already in these pages. Here are some more.

Flowers

❀ **Bugleweed** (*Ajuga*): Glossy easy-to grow perennial; use in rock garden or as ground cover. Blue flowers; green, variegated, or bronze leaves. Zone 2

❀ **Astilbe:** Likes moist soil; flowers are feathery spikes of red, lilac, pink, and white. Zone 4

❀ **Bleeding heart:** Ferny green foliage and rosy pink heart-shaped flowers in late spring; foliage disappears in summer so take note of where it's planted. Zone 3

❀ **Foxglove:** Can grow to 1.5 m to 2.5 m (5 to 8 feet) in very fertile soil; white, pink, brown, raspberry — many mouth-watering colours; biennial, so plant each year; some will self-seed. Zone 4

PRIMROSE: Give them moist soil; flower in spring in pink, white, yellow, red, purple, and every shade between. Zone 3

FORGET-ME-NOT: Annual with delicate blue, white, or pink flowers in spring and summer. Self-seeder in moist soil.

GROUND COVERS AND VINES

ENGLISH IVY: Perennial glossy vine or ground cover that grows well even in constant shade; holds leaves all winter. Zone 6

EUONYMUS: Perennial ground cover, vine, shrub, or small hedge. Leathery leaves stay on in winter. Zone 5

FOAMFLOWER: Perennial ground cover for a shady garden. Creeping plant with maple-like leaves, narrow clusters of small white flowers appear in spring. Keep well watered. Zone 3

JAPANESE SPURGE: Light green leaves make nice background for bulbs and help cover the dying foliage; perennial. Zone 3

PERIWINKLE: Shiny dark green leaves; blue, white, or purple; flowers in spring; perennial. Zone 3

HOSTA (my favourite!): Leaves available in various shades of greens with different textures; white or pale purple flowers; perennial. Zone 3.

Ground covers for the shade include ivy. English ivy is a perennial that holds its leaves all winter.

RULE OF THUMB:

Shade caused by a building is one thing. Shade from mature trees or shrubs is another. If you have to contend with the latter, remember the increased need for water, as roots compete for moisture. Plus, the quick depletion of organic matter in the soil results in a need for annual applications of finished compost or composted cattle manure — about 2.5 cm (1 inch) deep per year.

TREES AND SHRUBS

HEMLOCK: Can survive in constant shade. A good evergreen for clipping to suit the size of your garden. Zone 4

OREGON GRAPE: Shiny leaves shaped much like holly; yellow flowers give way to blue fruit; does much better in shade than in sun. Zone 5

RHODODENDRONS AND AZALEAS: Stay green in winter (although leaves will curl inwards in cold weather to conserve moisture). Frothy flowers in many colours and shades: pink, white, purple, yellow. Zone 5

REDBUD: Covered with pink flowers in spring. Zone 5

SASKATOON: Smothered in white flowers in spring; birds love the summer fruit. Zone 1

HIGHBUSH CRANBERRY: White flowers followed by bright red bitter fruit. Zone 2

ELDER: Flat creamy flower heads in spring give way to purple-black fruit. Zone 3

CARAGANA: Makes a good deciduous hedge with bright yellow, sweet-scented flowers in early summer. Zone 2

PLANTING TO ATTRACT BIRDS

Providing a welcoming habitat for birds enhances the joy of watching them in your garden. Even if you are generous in your offerings of food and water, you should also provide the birds with places to rest and in which to seek safety if they feel threatened. While you are planning your plantings, you might as well include some plants that birds are attracted to for food and shelter. Don't forget to check that the birds you want to attract are found in your region.

❋ Choose a variety of tall, medium, and low-growing plants and, if space permits, plant them in groupings. Some birds like to feed in the dense foliage at the top of a tree, others like the outer foliage.

❋ Variety in the height and group planting also provide shelter from the ground up in bad weather.

❋ Create a wild corner of your garden — use blackberries, raspberries, and honeysuckle with a wild rose to make a nesting thicket for birds such as finches and sparrows. Dense evergreen hedges of conifers also attract nesting birds such as the mourning dove, blue jay, finches, and sparrows.

SOME SUGGESTIONS

TO ATTRACT	PLANT
BALTIMORE (northern) ORIOLE	Highbush blueberry, wild cherry, red mulberry, serviceberry
BLACK-CAPPED CHICKADEE	Bayberry, birch, hemlock, pine, serviceberry, sunflower, winterberry, viburnum
BLUE JAY	Blackberry, blueberry, wild cherry, wild grape, holly, red mulberry, oak, sumac, sunflower, viburnum

PLANTS

CARDINAL	Wild cherry, dogwood, elderberry, hackberry, holly, red mulberry, sumac, viburnum
CEDAR WAXWING	Mountain ash, bayberry, blackberry, cedar (red and white), wild cherry, crabapple, dogwood, elderberry, hackberry, hawthorn, holly, red mulberry, serviceberry, viburnum, Virginia creeper
DARK-EYED JUNCO	Birch, fir, hemlock, honeysuckle, pine, sumac, tamarack
DOWNY WOODPECKER	Mountain ash, dogwood, mountain ash, oak, serviceberry, wild strawberry, Virginia creeper
EASTERN BLUEBIRD	Red cedar, dogwood, elderberry, wild grape, hackberry, holly, serviceberry, sumac, Virginia creeper
EASTERN MEADOWLARK	Blackberry, wild strawberry, sunflower
FLICKER	Dogwood, wild cherry, hackberry, oak, pine, serviceberry, wild strawberry, sumac, viburnum
GOLDFINCH	Alder, aster, birch, hemlock, honeysuckle, maple, oak, pine, spruce, sunflower, western sycamore, tamarack, cedar
HOUSE FINCH	Elderberry, grasses (for nesting), honeysuckle, pine, sumac, western sycamore
HOUSE WREN	Grasses (for nesting), oak, poplar
INDIGO BUNTING	Aster, elderberry, grasses (for nesting)
MOUNTAIN CHICKADEE	Oak, pine, sunflower
PYGMY NUTHATCH	Fir, pine
RED-HEADED WOODPECKER	Blackberry, dogwood, elderberry, oak, serviceberries
ROBIN	Mountain ash, bayberry, blackberry, red cedar, wild cherry,

	dogwood, elderberry, grasses (for nesting), hackberry, hawthorn, holly, red mulberry, serviceberry, sumac, viburnum
RUBY-THROATED HUMMINGBIRD	Bee balm, columbine, scarlet lobelia, trumpet vine
SCARLET TANAGER	Bayberry, blackberry, highbush blueberry, wild cherry, dogwood, elderberry, red mulberry, serviceberry, sumac
SONG SPARROW	Blackberry, highbush blueberry, wild cherry, elderberry, sunflower, Virginia creeper
STELLER'S JAY	Wild cherry, dogwood, elderberry, oak, pine, western raspberry, wild strawberry
WHITE-BREASTED NUTHATCH	Elderberry, maple, oak, pine, sunflower
WHITE-THROATED SPARROW	Red cedar, dogwood, elderberry, wild grape, holly, honeysuckle, maple, oak

GROUND COVERS

· · · · · · · · · · · · · · · · · · · ·

G ardens often have those maddening little spots that we just don't know what to do with — the space between a walk and the side of the house, the area beneath a huge spruce tree, a slope that needs stabilizing. These spaces can provide a transition between one part of the garden and the other. As well, use this space to add textures through plantings. Ground covers keep down weeds and hide ripening bulb foliage, just two of the roles for these useful garden plants.

❋ Choose from evergreen or deciduous plants, perennials or annuals. Look for plants that are low-growing and dense — and attractive! This might sound like a difficult bill to fill, but it is not at all. Just ask at your garden centre.

❋ If the area is one that gets walked or played on, ground covers might not be the answer. They just won't stand up to the wear and tear that grass can sustain.

❋ Some ground covers, such as violets and goutweed, can become invasive. If the plant you have chosen has this tendency, be sure the spot where you are planting it has some well-defined boundaries, such as between a driveway and a sidewalk.

❈ Refer to the sections in chapters 1 and 2, *Annuals* and *Perennials* on buying, planting, and caring for these plants. Ground covers are no different than other plants — they need weeding (though once they become well-established, weeding will become less frequent), watering, mulching, and some pruning now and then.

❈ For shade, choose euonymus, ivy, Japanese spurge, lamium, lily of the valley, and green goutweed.

❈ Some annual plants that can be used as ground covers are Iceland or California poppy and portulaca (sun), and impatiens (shade). Sedum and thyme (sun), both perennials, can also be used.

In a damp or shaded location ferns are a good choice for ground cover.

Here are some ground covers. All plants listed are perennials.

BARRENWORT *Epimedium*
Good on rocky slopes

COLOUR: Dainty pink, white, violet, yellow flowers appear from mid spring to early summer; pretty green foliage that turns dry reddish brown in winter.

ZONE: To Zone 3

HEIGHT: 30 cm (12 inches)

CULTIVATION TIPS: Sun or partial shade in well-drained humus-rich soil that keeps its moisture; makes a good contrast to ferns and hostas; does well under trees.

HEART-LEAVED BERGENIA *Bergenia cordifolia*
Flowers best in cooler zones

COLOUR: Mauve, red, pink, or white in spring; foliage is lustrous, leathery, and lettuce-like. It over winters like an evergreen and is one of the first perennials to grow come spring.

ZONE: To Zone 3

HEIGHT: 45 cm (18 inches)

CULTIVATION TIPS: Full sun with some afternoon shade if possible; moist, fertile humus-rich soil; trim leaves back in winter if they have turned brown.

CANDYTUFT *Iberis sempervirens*
Perennial evergreen in warm zones

COLOUR: Long-lasting white flowers in late spring; narrow evergreen leaves.

ZONE: To Zone 3

HEIGHT: 30 cm (12 inches)

CULTIVATION TIPS: Moist rich soil; cut back after flowering; looks good combined with spring bulbs. To get a second flowering, cut back 7.5 cm to 10 cm (3 to 4 inches) after spring blossoms are finished.

This ground cover, Geranium macrorrhizan, is very pretty with its pink flowers.

THREE-TOOTHED CINQUEFOIL *Potentilla tridentata*
For rocky, dry, sunny slopes

COLOUR: Small white flowers in early summer like those on strawberries; leaves are deep green and fan-shaped; remain attractive during the season; in fall, they turn dark red before dropping.

ZONE: To Zone 2

HEIGHT: 15 cm to 30 cm (6 to 12 inches)

CULTIVATION TIPS: Full sun in dry acid soil. Spreads in spite of dry conditions. Needs water during drought.

SPOTTED LAMIUM *Lamium maculatum*
Brightens a shade spot

COLOUR: Purple-pink flower spikes in late spring, early summer; foliage is silver and green and stays attractive throughout the season.

ZONE: To Zone 3

HEIGHT: 15 cm (6 inches)

CULTIVATION TIPS: Light to medium shade; moist, well-drained soil. Trim back in summer if it becomes lanky; water during dry spells.

77

LILY OF THE VALLEY   *Convallaria majalis*
Invasive, but sweet-scented

COLOUR: Scented white bell-shaped flowers in spring, followed by red berries, which are poisonous.
ZONE: To Zone 3
HEIGHT: 20 cm (8 inches)
CULTIVATION TIPS: Likes moist soil and partial shade; in heavy shade it will not produce as many flowers; looks nice planted with hostas. Cut flowers for tiny bouquets.

CREEPING PHLOX   *Phlox stolonifera*
Evergreen for shade

COLOUR: Lavish blue, pink, or white flowers in spring.
ZONE: To Zone 2
HEIGHT: 30 cm (12 inches)
CULTIVATION TIPS: Light to medium shade in moist rich soil; deadhead with garden shears after flowering; water during drought.

WILD STRAWBERRY   *Fragaria virginia*
Bonus: you get edible berries

COLOUR: White blossoms give way to red fruits; shiny evergreen leaves.
ZONE: To Zone 4
HEIGHT: 15 cm to 20 cm (6 to 8 inches)
CULTIVATION TIPS: Full sun, average well-drained soil; spreads by runners; the birds might get the berries before you do.

VIRGINIA CREEPER   *Parthenocissus quinquefolia*
Lovely fall colour

COLOUR: Green foliage turns bright red in fall; small white or green flowers turn into blue-black grape-like berries in fall.
ZONE: To Zone 2
HEIGHT: Can cover an area 15 m (50 feet)

CULTIVATION TIPS: Full sun to full shade. Grows
quickly, tolerates urban environment.

....

WINTERGREEN *Gaultheria procumbens*
Red berries in the fall

COLOUR: Evergreen dark green leaves that turn red in
cold; pink-white flowers all summer; red fruit
throughout winter.
ZONE: To Zone 3
HEIGHT: 60 cm (2 feet)
CULTIVATION TIPS: Acid soil; keep well-watered; full
sun or light to medium shade.

....

SWEET WOODRUFF *Galium odoratum*
Fragrant flowers

COLOUR: Small white flowers in spring; green foliage
stays attractive to fall.
ZONE: To Zone 3
HEIGHT: 10 cm to 22 cm (4 to 9 inches)
CULTIVATION TIPS: Light to medium shade; moist soil;
may disappear in hot humid weather but will return
when weather cools, so not ideal as ground cover in
some areas of the country; makes a nice companion to
white-flowered azaleas or yellow and white daffodils.

*Wild Ginger is another type of ground cover. It is a good
choice for the wildflower garden.*

GRASS

Finally, don't forget the most often used ground cover of all — grass. It is the answer for sunny, well-travelled spots in the garden. Grass makes lawns, and lawns are the carpet of our outdoor rooms. Grass provides softness to the feet and comfort to the eye. It provides a canvas for the passing seasons — in spring, its green is patterned with the outlines of branches; in winter, the white expanse shows off the same shadows; in summer, it reflects the movement of the surrounding trees, effectively cooling the environment; and in autumn, it offers a foil for the multi-coloured leaves that fall on it.

Grass makes the lawn one of the most intensely planted areas of the garden and, as such, needs some special care.

❄ In the spring, rake established lawns lightly to remove winter debris. Repair any bare patches with topsoil and seed, or patches of sod. Fertilize with a slow-release fertilizer such as 21-7-7. A slow-release urea fertilizer will not burn your garden and can be applied in early and late spring. Another fertilizer application can be made in the middle of the summer, but it should be a low-nitrogen type such as a slow-release 10-6-4. Don't apply it during very dry weather.

❄ When you cut the grass, keep the blades of the mower set high so that the grass is always at least 5 cm (2 inches) high. This helps to keep weeds under control and helps protect the roots. They don't dry out as quickly as when the grass is shorter. If you want to rake the clippings, add them to the compost or let them dry before using them as mulch. If you cut the grass frequently, the clippings will be fairly short and can be left where they fall. Cut the grass when it seems to need it. Grass doesn't grow according to a schedule! There are times it will grow quickly (in cool, moist weather) and times it will grow much more slowly. I recommend using mulching mowers.

Watering is another lawn-care task that usually can't be done according to a preordained schedule. Weather is the guide here. Lawns need about 2.5 cm (1 inch) of water a week during times of drought or low rainfall. Windy weather also dries out a lawn. In a prolonged spell of hot dry windy weather, you may well want to institute a weekly watering schedule.

If any weeds appear in spite of high mowing, deal with them by hand at once.

RULE OF THUMB:

I have three rules of thumb for your lawn:

1. Don't scalp your lawn or try to imitate the look of your favourite golf course (unless you want the intense maintenance schedule of one!). The taller the grass, the deeper the roots. Remember to cut your lawn no lower than 5 cm (2 inches). Your lawn will be thicker, greener, and more drought tolerant. More time for you to golf or whatever!

2. Mulch. Most power mowers offer the option to mulch grass clippings — take it! You will never rake your lawn clippings again; your lawn will not accumulate thatch (dead stolons and grass stems) and the clippings return nitrogen to your lawn to the extent that you can eliminate one application of fertilizer per year. Wow!

3. Strangle weeds out of existence by overseeding your lawn with good-quality grass seed. Spread seed over finished compost or a soilless mix designed for lawn-seed starting.

❊ If crabgrass is a problem in your area, treat the lawn with a pre-emergent weed killer early in the spring, usually applied in combination with a granular lawn fertilizer.

❊ Grubs can sometimes become a problem. They feed on the roots of grass, causing the plant to die. Look for brown patches and pull at the affected plants. If they come away in your hand, you probably have grubs in your lawn. Use an insecticide formulated to eradicate grubs, following directions carefully, or take the effective, environmentally friendly approach and apply the new dormant beneficial nematodes now on the market. If the grass doesn't come away in your hand but is still brown, the chinch bug is probably doing the damage. Endophyte-enhanced lawn seed is helpful in bringing chinch bug and sod webworm under control.

❊ Some diseases that affect grass are snow mould and powdery mildew. Both are funguses and are usually temporary conditions. Snow mould occurs on parts of the lawn that have northern exposures. It starts as small straw-coloured spots on the grass, which turn into crusty mats. Break up the threads of the mat with the rake as soon as you notice them and your grass is likely to recover. It is possible to control mildew with a fungicide, but it often disappears on its own in cool dry weather.

❊ In September or October, give the lawn a final feeding with fall fertilizer. Keep cutting the grass until it stops growing. Because rainfall often increases in the autumn, the grass will grow quite lushly, so you will probably be mowing more frequently than you did all summer!

❊ Keep the lawn raked, especially as leaves start to fall. Leaves left on grass over winter can become a sodden, impenetrable mat, harbouring diseases and insects and damaging the grass beneath.

NATIVE FLOWERS

As our sophistication as gardeners increases, we become aware of the allure of using plants native to Canada. When we use plants native to our region, we know that they will grow in the conditions in our particular part of Canada. They will survive without a lot of coddling. Don't confine yourself to flowers, shrubs, and trees, though. Grasses used as accents add a lovely element in the garden and many have a part to play in the winter garden, where they help trap snow and provide some colour.

I have given the ranges where these plants are native as a guideline for deciding which plants will be at home in your garden. However, plants don't always conveniently grow within geographic boundaries, so if you think you have similar growing conditions, give them a try.

These garden lupines are a descendant of the wild lupine, a flower native to Canada.

Black-eyed Susan (*Rudbeckia hirta*). Easy to grow, especially in the east and on the prairies. Orange-yellow flowers with bronze-black centre in summer. Height 60 cm to 69 cm (2 to 3 feet). Habitat: Fields, prairies, and open woods. Range: Throughout Canada.

Blazing Star (*Liatris punctata*). Spikes of rosy-purple flowers in summer. Full sun, well-drained, fairly fertile soil. Height 60 cm to 180 cm (2 to 6 feet). Habitat: Dry prairies. Range: Manitoba.

Bloodroot (*Sanguinaria canadensis*). White small flowers in March to May. Roots and stems have a red-orange juice. Goes dormant in a dry summer. Height 15 cm to 30 cm (6 to 12 inches). Habitat: Rich woodlands, along streams. Range: Across Canada to Nova Scotia.

Butterfly weed (*Asclepias tuberosa*). Small bright orange clusters of flowers in June to September. Height: 30 cm to 75 cm (12 to 30 inches). Habitat: Dry open soil, roadsides, fields. Range: Ontario to Newfoundland.

Black-eyed Susan is found throughout Canada. It is a charming addition to borders and beds.

❀
PURPLE CACTUS (*Mamillaria vivipara*). Purple flowers on spiny plants in early summer. Height 2.5 cm to 7.5 cm (1 to 3 inches). Habitat: Open prairie and hillsides. Range: Manitoba, Saskatchewan, and Alberta.

❀
FOAMFLOWER (*Tiarella cordifolia*). Small white flowers in a feathery cluster in April to June. Height: 15 cm to 30 cm (6 to 12 inches). Habitat: Rich woods. Range: Ontario to Nova Scotia.

❀
WILD GRAPE (*Vitis riparia*). Small green flowers in late spring to early summer turn into shiny black grapes. Sun or partial shade in a moist well-drained location. Habitat: Stream banks. Region: New Brunswick, Quebec, Manitoba.

❀
HAREBELL (*Campanula rotundifolia*). Blue bluebell-like flowers on dainty stems from June to September. Height 15 cm to 50 cm (6 to 20 inches). Habitat: Rocky banks and slopes, meadows, alpine areas. Range: Northern Canada south through to the United States.

❀
HEPATICA (*Hepatica acutiloba*). Pink, lavender-blue, or white flowers in March to June. Prefers soil rich in calcium. Height: 10 cm to 15 cm (4 to 6 inches). Habitat: Dry rocky woods. Range: Manitoba to Nova Scotia.

❀
CANADA LILY (*Lilium canadense*). Yellow to orange-red flowers with dark spots. Height 60 cm to 150 cm (2 to 5 feet). Habitat: Wet meadows, woodlands, and borders. Range: Ontario, Quebec, and Nova Scotia.

❀
WILD LUPINE (*Lupinus*). Flower spikes of blue, pink, or white and downy stems. Height 30 cm to 120 cm (1 to 4 feet). Habitat: Dry open woods and fields. Range: Across Canada.

VINES AND CLIMBERS

●●●●●●●●●●●●●●●●●●●●●●●

D o you have a wall that looks a little lonely? Does the view of the next-door neighbour's rusty car irritate you? Are you gardening on a small balcony but want to grow more and more? I will tell you the answer to these gardening problems — vines and climbing plants.

Annuals, perennials, evergreen, deciduous — climbers and vines come in the same wide range as other garden plants, but they need something to climb on. It is important to know what kind of climber they are so you can provide the correct support for your particular choices.

❋ Tendrils: small tendrils grow from the stem or other part of the plant and twine themselves around the host. Example: sweet peas

❋ Twining leafstalks: the leafstalks twine themselves around the host. Example: clematis

❋ Twining stems: the stem of the whole plant twines itself around the host. Example: morning glory

❋ Clinging roots: as the plant grows, small roots are formed on the new growth, attaching themselves to the host. Example: English ivy

How They Grow:
Different Forms of
Climbers and Vines.

Tendril form   *Twining leafstalk*

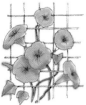

Twining stem   *Clinging disc*

❋ Clinging discs: small pads on new growth attach themselves to the host. Example: Virginia creeper

❋ Climbing roses. They fit into none of the above types, but climbing roses also need a little help. Either grow them on a lattice of some sort or provide anchors in the wall through which you can thread twist ties to loosely hold the stems in place. If you use a lattice, carefully guide stems through the holes in the lattice; the thorns will help keep the stems and branches in place.

PLANTING TIPS

❋ A plant that grows against any wall, except a north-facing one, will initially need extra watering as it will be affected by the heat absorbed and reflected by the wall.

❋ When planting vines next to a wall, place the stem 15 cm to 30 cm (6 to 12 inches) away from the wall. Fan the roots outward, away from the wall. This will ensure that they get sufficient moisture.

❋ The height of the vine is often governed by the height of its support.

This trellis forms a strong support for the clematis.

SOME VINES TO CONSIDER

....

CLEMATIS   *Clematis*
Masses of beautiful flowers late spring through summer

ZONE: Zone 2, depending on variety

HEIGHT: To 3.5 m (12 feet) depending on variety

CULTIVATION: Roots should be shaded, either by another plant or a stone; rest of plant needs 5 to 6 hours of sun; prefers alkaline soil to acid; soil should also be porous, fertile, and moisture-retentive. Plants are pruned according to when they flower; those that bloom in late spring and early summer on old wood and in late summer on new wood are lightly pruned after first flowering; those that bloom in late summer on new wood are pruned in the spring to within 60 cm (2 feet) of the ground; native clematis needs no pruning.

COMMENTS: Perennial vine; available in a wide range of colours — pure white, blue, purple, red, pink, as well as some combined colours — and flower sizes, as well as flowering periods — from May to September.

VIRGINIA CREEPER   *Parthenocissus quinquefolia*
Brilliant fall colour

ZONE: Zone 2
HEIGHT: 21 m (70 feet)
CULTIVATION: Moist, loamy soil, not too acid
COMMENTS: Perennial; deciduous and self-supporting.
Can become invasive. Green leaves turn brilliant
scarlet in autumn.

EUONYMUS   *Euonymus fortunei*
Reliable evergreen

ZONE: Zone 4
HEIGHT: 3 m to 12 m (10 to 40 feet)
CULTIVATION: Ordinary soil in sun or partial shade
COMMENTS: Evergreen rambler. Grow up a tree or
over a fence or wall.

GRAPES   *Vita*
Fast growing, fruiting

ZONE: To Zone 3
HEIGHT: 2.5 m to 3.5 m (8 to 12 feet)
CULTIVATION: Sunny spot, well-drained soil; tolerant
of slight clay conditions
COMMENTS: Requires support (twining vine); provides
habitat and food for birds; hybrid varieties not as
hardy as species types.

CLIMBING HYDRANGEA   *Hydrangea petiolaris*
Wonderful on shady wall

ZONE: Zone 5
HEIGHT: 18 m to 24 m (60 to 80 feet)
CULTIVATION: Sun or shade; rich well-drained soil
COMMENTS: Deciduous; perennial; adhering roots.
Flowers are white, lacy, and scented; leaves are
glossy, stems are strong. Flowerheads left on the
plant turn brown and look nice in winter. Cover
walls, arbours, trees.

....

CLIMBING ROSE   *Rosa*
Masses of scented of blooms

ZONE: Zone
HEIGHT: 3 m to 9 m (10 to 30 feet)
CULTIVATION: Full sun, although in very hot areas, some afternoon protection is desirable. Well-drained soil is a must and if it's slightly acid, so much the better.
COMMENTS: Perennial, deciduous. Considered weavers rather than twiners, they produce flexible stems that must be attached to a host or threaded through openings in lattice by the gardener; the thorns help keep them in position once there. Training the branches horizontally makes them produce more blooms.

Climbing roses are simply magnificent. Consider how the look of your home could be changed by adding climbing roses to a wall, fence, or balcony railing.

WISTERIA   *Wisteria*
Dramatic and old-fashioned

ZONE: Zone 4

HEIGHT: 6 m to 12 m (20 to 40 feet)

CULTIVATION: Full sun is vital for flowering; well-drained soil. A weak soil will encourage blossoms; soils high in nitrogen will give lots of foliage and little bloom.

COMMENTS: Perennial, deciduous twiner. Flowers are lilac, pink, pink and white, and purple. Strong support needed for this quick and long-living grower. The biggest complaint I've heard with wisteria is the number of years after planting it takes to bloom. The most effective and fastest way to get it to bloom that I have seen is training a wisteria on a series of wires on a south facing, light coloured, brick wall. The effect was fast (within three years) and magnificent. Also, adding super phosphate fertilizer (0-20-0) to the soil or root pruning can get a non-bloomer to form flower buds.

RULE OF THUMB:

Walls, fences, railings, and other verticals offer the perfect area to begin your garden. Any vertical space in your yard or balcony provides an opportunity to enjoy all the benefits of gardening by planting vines. Kids can get a start at gardening by sowing their own morning glory seeds; these plants are tolerant of poor soil and grow quickly. For fruit, you cannot beat grape vines. For colour, review the above list.

COTTAGE GARDENS

First, check out the zone your cottage is in if you plan to plant perennials. It is likely to be different than the one at home, and usually it's colder.

PLANTS

❀ Container gardening is often the answer at the cottage where competition from tree roots is not a problem. Use the polymer crystals that absorb water and release it as needed.

❀ Use easy-care ground covers — you don't want to spoil the tranquillity of the cottage with a noisy lawnmower. Native ferns make beautiful cottage ground covers.

❀ Keep the use of chemicals to a minimum. Topsoil is often very shallow and any chemical addition can quickly leach into the water.

❀ Many cottages are situated in rocky parts of Canada. Take advantage by building a natural rock garden. Place soil into cracks, crevices, and pockets in the rocks and then pop in the plants. Check the section on rock gardens in Chapter 3.

❀ Some easy-care, drought-tolerant perennials: aster, spurge, sedums, bugleweed, common thrift, coreopsis, shooting star, coneflower, statice, sundrop, beardtongue, bear's breech, rock cress, butterfly weed, honeysuckle, and grapes. Some easy-care drought-tolerant annuals: aster, bachelor button, lupine, cosmos, Chinese lanterns, hollyhock, feverfew, and portulaca.

❀ If your summer getaway is by the sea, look for plants that are salt-tolerant, prefer sandy soils, and will hold moisture under windy conditions. If you enrich sandy soil with generous quantities of compost, annuals such as the following will do well: cornflowers, nasturtiums, petunias, and portulaca. Plant a permanent tall hedge to act as a windbreak so you can expand the range of plants you grow — hollyhocks, foxgloves, Canterbury bells, iris, Oriental poppies, delphiniums, daylilies, phlox, columbine, peonies and, if well-protected from salt spray and high winds, roses and hydrangeas.

HERITAGE GARDENS

When I drive into the country, I sometimes see stands of lilacs or sweeps of orange daylilies in the middle of a field. Right away I know a farmhouse used to exist there. These are reminders of successful gardens from years gone by.

There is a great appeal in these plants and there are several reasons why they are still popular. They are beautiful, for starters. They also are bothered by few diseases and insects. As well, they are flexible and will grow in many regions of the country.

Heritage gardens should look as if they have been there forever, and that means the style of your house should complement the garden. A heritage garden is not usually a garden for a new house, especially a very modern-looking one. If you have a new house and you dream of a heritage garden, start by preparing a "background." That is, plant some vines to grow up the walls of your house, such as honeysuckle and climbing roses, to soften its lines. As the years pass, gradually add some heritage plants as the vines and background plants fill in.

DAYLILIES: Orange yellow, rusty red, pink, burgundy. Bloom appears from June to August.

DELPHINIUM: Rich blue, white, yellow, pink, purple, and red flowers in June. Staking almost always a must.

FOXGLOVE: Creamy-white, yellow, apricot, chocolate-brown, many shades of pink.

LILAC: A true heritage shrub — early settlers

packed cuttings in their baggage to bring to the New Country. Blooms in deep purple, pale mauve, creamy white — and scented!

LUPIN: Tall spikes covered with pea-like flowers in blue, pink, red, purple, salmon.

PEONY: Noted for their long lives and hardiness. Blooms in May and June in pink, yellow, red, white flowers.

PHLOX   (*Phlox paniculata*): Use in the native garden as well — it is native to North America. Colours from white through pink, red, lavender and purple.

RAMBLING AND CLIMBING ROSES: Let them ramble over fences, arbours, porches, verandahs for a truly old-fashioned look. Some lovely climbers have been developed in Canada for our weather conditions — they are the heirloom plants of tomorrow.

SWEET PEAS: Lovely pastel colours — white, lilac, pink, mauve — but some vibrant reds, blues, and burgundies.

Delphinium, my mother's favourite flower, is a beautiful way to add a vertical flowering element to the border.

INDEX

See all 4 volumes in *The Complete Gardener* series:

Simplifies the process of design and demystifies the issue of colour. Essential information for planning your garden so it looks its best. Includes planting instructions on making your own all-white garden regardless of your garden size. Accompanied by video.

Learn how to add interest and charm through the furnishings in your garden. From arbours to urns—they're here! Features step-by-step directions for making and planting a "stone" trough that would cost a small fortune to buy! Accompanied by video.

These fundamentals of good gardening practice will help you to create and keep a garden full of blooming, healthy plants. Don't miss the recipe for compost tea—your plants will love it! Accompanied by video.

Helps you select the best annuals, perennials, vines, ground covers, trees and shrubs and bulbs for your growing conditions. Special instructions on how to plant a beautiful four-season window box. Accompanied by video.